IPS

Dubious Specter

A Skeptical Look at the Soviet Nuclear Threat

Fred M. Kaplan

The Institute for Policy Studies is a non-partisan research institute. The views expressed in this study are solely those of the author.

© 1980 Fred M. Kaplan

Published by the Institute for Policy Studies.

Copies of this book are available from the Institute for Policy Studies, 1901 Q Street, N.W., Washington, D.C. 20009 or Paulus Potterstraat 20, 1071 DA, Amsterdam, Holland.

Third Printing: 1982
Revised Second Printing: 1980
First Printing: 1977
Library of Congress Catalog Number 80-50894
ISBN 0-89758-023-0

ABOUT THE AUTHOR

FRED KAPLAN has written on defense and foreign policy issues for *The New York Times Magazine, Scientific American, Der Spiegel, The Nation, Bulletin of the Atomic Scientists* and other publications. He received a B.A. in government from Oberlin College and a Master's in political science from M.I.T., where he is presently a Ph.D. candidate and a fellow (on-leave) of the Arms Control Project of M.I.T.'s Center for International Studies.

Currently defense-policy advisor to Rep. Les Aspin in the U.S. House of Representatives, he has also worked at the Carnegie Endowment for International Peace and the Institute for Policy Studies.

TABLE OF CONTENTS

PREFACE TO
SECOND EDITION

First, a few words on what this monograph is *not*. It is not about the Soviet invasion of Afghanistan, Soviet motives in the Persian Gulf, or the balance of military power in Europe. It is not an apology for the Soviet Union's leaders, domestic politics or foreign policy, none of which I find at all admirable.

This small book *is* about the strategic nuclear balance between the United States and the Soviet Union—and, implicitly, about whether the state of this balance, for now and in the foreseeable future, has any implications for international politics broadly speaking. It analyzes the increasingly widespread contention that the Soviet Union's strategic nuclear forces are "superior" to those of the United States and that the Soviets are aiming to fight and win a nuclear war. My aim is to challenge and try to dispel some hard-worn myths that have recently gained an extraordinary amount of attention—and, in turn public credence—and to put some widely publicized facts into a broader perspective. At the same time, I summarize and examine some basic issues of defense policy and strategy, which have been badly misunderstood by many analysts (on the left, right and center) and without which a discussion of something called a "military balance" is pointless and abstract.

This is the second edition of this monograph. Although my basic conclusions are the same, this edition constitutes a major revision. First, I have updated the data. Second, with the SALT II debate (and its recent shelving), it is obviously appropriate to deal with the future of arms control at some length. Third, the defense debate has taken a few turns in the past two-and-a-half years and I have re-directed this new edition accordingly. For example, when I wrote the first edition, many people were worrying about the "throw-weight" of Soviet "heavy missiles," so I devoted a good deal of attention to whether this measure had any military significance. Since then, the growing accuracy of these Soviet missiles (a fairly recent trend)—along with a growing fear that our own

land-based missiles are becoming vulnerable to attack—
has become the major issue in the strategic debate; so in
this edition, I devote quite a bit of space to examining the
rather bizarre scenarios surrounding this fear. Finally, I
have added some more information and a slightly
different perspective on the evolution of American
defense strategy. All in all, the second edition is in many
ways an entirely different booklet from the first.

In any event, I thank Stephen Daggett and Michael
Klare of the Institute for Policy Studies for asking me to
write this second edition and, once again, Richard Barnet
and Marcus Raskin for suggesting that I write the first
one.

— Fred Kaplan
Washington, D.C.
February 1980

I.
INTRODUCTION: AMERICAN NUCLEAR STRATEGY

After a long, mostly tranquil period of peaceful coexistence, summitry, wheat sales, and an American body politic preoccupied with domestic issues, the Soviet Threat Assessment business is booming again. Alarming portraits of Soviet missile threats are once more in vogue. Indeed, the new phase in the nuclear arms race and the latest deterioration in Soviet-American relations has stirred the liveliest excitement in the defense world since the famous, but subsequently disproved, "missile gap" syndrome of the late 1950s.

The renaissance of pessimistic defense analysis springs largely from widespread claims that the USSR is aiming for "strategic superiority" and will get there by the early to mid-1980s. This prognosis has so pervasively and almost routinely been reported in the mass media that it is rapidly becoming commonplace, the hard-headed new realism for a hard-boiled age.

Often overlooked in popular discussions of the Soviet threat is its relation to U.S. strategy. And yet discussion of the Soviet threat and the strategic balance makes no sense without an understanding of American nuclear strategy. Strategy, after all, concerns the purpose of a military force, the missions it is designed to perform, how it is to be used. Military threats and the military balance are assessed on the basis of whether, or to what extent, one side can prevent the other from performing its missions, that is, from implementing its strategy. In short, the strategy, the balance and the threat all hinge on

1

one another, and cannot be considered independently in any meaningful fashion.

During the Eisenhower period of the 1950s, the United States officially pursued a strategy of Massive Retaliation: any Communist provocation would be countered with a devastating blow, completely wiping out Soviet or Chinese society. This certainly would be a sure deterrent to Communist adventurism. However, no specific requirements for such a response were set down: What does "massive" mean? How much was needed to deter? And what sorts of threats would this power deter—all types or just the threat of nuclear attack?

In short, aside from the vague "Massive Retaliation" catch-all, there were no means to develop a broad, overarching national strategy concerning these weapons, no coordinating body that could calculate *how much of what* was needed to carry out *what sort of policy,* for specifically *what sorts of aims.* The three armed services operated autonomously, and each built up its own nuclear arsenal. The bureaucracy arrived at arms budgets irrationally, chiefly through internecine wrangling within arbitrary spending ceilings. Many different views were held throughout the government—but no single view. Some sophisticated ideas came out of the RAND Corporation in Santa Monica and other government-contracted think-tanks, and sometimes they were influential. But there was neither the consistent set of intellectual concepts nor the centralized administrative apparatus necessary for planning and designing forces according to any principle of strategy.

In the Kennedy and Johnson Administrations, Defense Secretary Robert McNamara—former president of Ford Motors, a businessman with a strong quantitative bent—changed all this. He established a Systems Analysis office, and filled its ranks with "whiz kids" from RAND. He centralized defense planning, forced a thorough consideration of the specific nature of American objectives, and attempted—at least theoretically—to plan and restrict weapons developments to the point where these objectives could be attained, and no further. Planning was done under conservative assumptions (against a hypothetical "greater-than-expected threat"),

2

but there *was* planning.[1]

The official policy that emerged from all this became known as "mutual deterrence" or "mutual assured destruction" (MAD, as some cynics dubbed it). The essence of MAD was that neither superpower would strike first with nuclear weapons, knowing that it would be destroyed by the other in a devastating retaliatory blow. The whiz kids even calculated how much it would take to deter: they figured that the task required marshalling sufficient blast power to kill about 25 percent of the Soviet population (not including deaths caused by radiation, fallout and other incalculable long-term effects of nuclear weapons) and to destroy 50 to 60 percent of its industry. To accomplish this awesome task would, they calculated, require the equivalent of 400 one-megaton bombs. They later refined this view to read that each "leg" of the "Strategic Triad"—the tripartite arsenal composed of land-based intercontinental ballistic missiles (ICBMs), submarine-launched ballistic missiles (SLBMs) and intercontinental bombers—should be able, *independently,* to carry out this task (so that each could produce the requisite damage in čase the other two legs failed or were destroyed).

This formula constituted an important—though never fully accepted—transformation in U.S. policy. Its implications were later summed up by two of McNamara's top systems analysts:

> U.S. weapons should be measured against U.S. objectives, not against Soviet objectives . . . The important question is not total megatons or numbers of delivery systems or any other single measure of strategic nuclear capability, but *whether U.S. forces can effectively carry out their missions. Once we are sure that, in retaliation, we can destroy the Soviet Union and other potential attackers as modern societies, we cannot increase our security or power against them by threatening to destroy more.*[2]

Thus was born the concept of *finite deterrence*—deterrence is maintained, so goes the argument, as long as the United States has enough missiles and bombers with

3

which to retaliate devastatingly in the event of enemy attack; any additional weaponry would not, according to this logic, add anything to U.S. security. By 1967, having amassed 1054 ICBMs, 656 SLBMs on 41 nuclear-missile submarines, and about 600 long-range bombers, the Defense Department explicitly decided that *that* was enough. (In fact, the United States has, since then, further reduced its number of bombers to 348.)[3]

All of this sounded highly scientific, and indeed it was more systematic than the Eisenhower/Dulles "Massive Retaliation" policy which it replaced; but the basis for the "assured destruction" formula was more arbitrary than rational. The calculation for the requirements of deterrence—400 equivalent megatons, 25 percent of population killed, 50 percent of industry destroyed—was based not on an intensive analysis of the Soviet economic infrastructure, nor on psychology, sociology, Kremlinology or anything of the sort. Rather, it was "influenced by the fact of strongly diminishing marginal returns."[4] That is, after the blast equivalent of 400 one-megaton bombs, the amount of destruction wreaked by any additional weapons is, on the margin, minimal. And it just so happens that the destructive curve begins to flatten out dramatically at the point where 25 to 30 percent of the Soviet population and 50 or so percent of its industry are destroyed. (See Figure 1.)

Recent research by defense analyst Kevin Lewis reveals that the 400-equivalent-megaton requirement may have been even more arbitrary, based simply on the destructive power of the forces that McNamara had already planned to procure. Taking into account reliability and alert rates, it just so happened that the U.S. strategic forces of the early to mid 1960s would have, on each leg of the Triad, about 400 equivalent megatons. (See Figure 2.)[5]

This clever rationale was soon to collapse, however; for around that time, the U.S. began to develop, and in 1970 first deployed, missiles with multiple independently targetable re-entry vehicles (MIRVs), or multiple warheads. This move increased the number of nuclear weapons in the arsenal without involving an increase in the number of missiles. The Pentagon officially justified

FIGURE 1
"Soviet Population and Industry Destroyed by Megatons"*

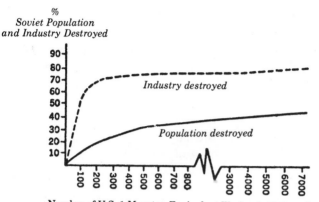

Number of U.S. 1 Megaton Equivalent Warheads Delivered

*Not including deaths caused by radiation, fallout or firestorm.

Source: "U.S. Strategic Offensive Forces in the 1960's," in Commission on the Organization of the Government for the Conduct of Foreign Policies, *Appendices,* Vol. 4, p. 139.

MIRVs as "penetration aids" in the event of a crash build-up by the Soviets in anti-ballistic missiles (ABMs). That is, if the Soviets could destroy in-coming warheads, we would need more of them so as to be able to saturate their ABM systems with some of the MIRVs while having enough left over to smash through the depleted defenses and hit the assigned targets. Yet when the ABM Treaty was signed at SALT I in May 1972, limiting each super-power to two ABM sites with no more than 100 missiles at each, the U.S. continued to build MIRVed missiles.

For the MIRVs were in fact devised chiefly as *counterforce* weapons—counterforce being a strategy for destroying military targets, such as war industries, air bases, nuclear-storage facilities, command posts, submarine ports and ICBM silos, in a limited nuclear war.

If the truth be told, McNamara had in mind a counter-

FIGURE 2

Weapon	#	Warheads/ Vehicle	EMT/* Warhead	r/a**	Total EMT
Polaris	41	16	1	.6 =	∼400
Minuteman	450	1	1	.9 =	∼400
B-52	300	4	1.3	.25 =	∼400

*Equivalent Megatons, or the 2/3 power of explosive yield.
**Reliability or availability of weapons. For Polaris, the number of subs constantly on station; for Minuteman, the number ready at all times; for B-52, the number on constant alert.

force strategy from the beginning.* So did most of his systems analysts, who had devised the concept while at RAND. All the talk about "assured destruction," "finite deterrence," and so on was mainly a ruse to prevent the military services from expanding the U.S. arsenal in wild proportions. It just so happened, by a nice coincidence, that 400 equivalent-megatons was not only the right number for "assured destruction"; it was also enough, at least in the early 1960s, to carry out all the counterforce options that McNamara wanted besides.[6]

In 1962, McNamara delivered a speech at Ann Arbor, often called the "no-cities" speech. In it, he proposed that the Americans and Russians agree that cities not be targeted in the event of nuclear war. The speech caused a fervor. The Soviets accused McNamara of being a dangerous warmonger who wanted to invent rules for the holocaust; arms controllers denounced him for violating deterrence theory ("mutual assured destruction"); and the Joint Chiefs of Staff and the Strategic Air Command (SAC) immediately presented a shopping list for the weapons they "needed" to prepare for this "limited

*"Counterforce" does not necessarily signify "first-strike," contrary to a popular impression—although, true, enough counterforce weapons could translate into a first-strike capability, whether this is the intention or not. It is doubtful that McNamara had in mind a first-strike strategy, otherwise why would he have spent so much money making the forces more "survivable" (starting the Polaris submarine, developing the solid-fuel Minuteman missile and encasing them in concrete, putting B52s on constant alert, etc.)?

6

A number of recent studies persuasively demonstrate that the Pentagon pursued a counterforce strategy from early on in the Kennedy Administration.

options/no-cities" strategy. The list included a greatly expanded Minuteman ICBM force (2000-2150 missiles by 1971), the development of warheads with very high yields (over 50 megatons for some) and very fine accuracy, a variety of "dial-a-yield" options for SLBM warheads, a force of bombers with "fully reprogrammable" cruise missiles and very high kill-probabilities against all targets, including missile silos, and more. This list grew out of an extensive study—the Hickey Study—conducted by the Defense Department in the Spring of 1961; the McNamara initiative provided the perfect opportunity for implementing it.[7]

The counterforce shopping list dismayed McNamara, the cost-controller, to no end. He immediately told the Joint Chiefs to pay no attention to his public remarks, that "assured destruction" still comprised the criterion for force planning, and that he would hear nothing more about all these improved counterforce weapons that they were asking for. For one thing, they simply were unnecessary at that time.[8]

Still, a number of recent studies persuasively demonstrate that the Pentagon pursued a counterforce strategy from early on in the Kennedy Administration.[9] In 1962, the Joint Strategic Targeting Staff, at SAC Headquarters in Omaha, drew up the first revised Single Integrated Operational Plan (SIOP, pronounced sigh-op). The SIOP is the set of targeting plans that SAC prepares for fighting a nuclear war. The plans are composed by military men, who naturally think about attacking militarily significant targets. Needless to say, residential areas or population *per se*—the natural targets of a "mutual assured destruction" strategy—were not on this list of targets. Rather, the list was—and still is—composed of military targets and high-value industrial facilities.

The SIOP of today has more refined features than the one of 1962, but they are essentially similar. As the

7

From the mid-1960s on, however, the United States expanded its nuclear arsenal—not so much to expand capabilities as to maintain counterforce targeting strategies.

current Defense Secretary, Harold Brown (also the Director of Defense Research and Engineering in the Kennedy Administration), recently testified, "We have never targeted populations as such. We have always targeted military and industrial objectives, and we have always targeted military targets." Further, "the ability to attack a variety of military targets has always been a *central* feature of our strategic force" both in "our strategy and . . . in our doctrine."[10] General David Jones, Chairman of the Joint Chiefs of Staff, agrees: "We have not in the past had a mutual assured destruction strategy."[11]

Thinking about counterforce originated out of repulsion against John Foster Dulles' strategy of Massive Retaliation. McNamara and his aides adopted the view, held by strategists at the RAND Corporation and other academic centers in the 1950s, that the Dulles policy lacked credibility, and that more flexible options were needed to respond to more limited threats—options providing, first, conventional military responses (in Western Europe for possible NATO-Warsaw Pact clashes and in the Third World for counterinsurgency expeditions) and, second, the ability to strike selectively at targets other than Soviet population centers in the event of "limited" nuclear strikes against the United States or its allies.[12]

In public, McNamara underplayed the significance of these flexible nuclear options, in part to control profligate spending by the armed services, and in part because of certain technological limitations of the day. From the mid-1960s on, however, the United States expanded its nuclear arsenal—not so much to expand capabilities as to maintain counterforce targeting strategies.

This was the basic motivation behind the deployment of multiple warheads. In 1962, the Soviet Union had about

30 ICBMs; by 1967 they had more than 500, and by 1969 more than 1000.[13] If the United States were to maintain counterforce options, the Defense Department had to expand the number of ICBM warheads—which it did through MIRVs as soon as the technology (already in development) could be militarily exploited and deployed. Similarly, in the late 1960s and again in the 1970s, the Soviets, following our prudent example, began "hardening" their missiles—i.e., encasing them in underground silos, pouring on layers of cement, and fixing them on shock-absorbers and springs. In response, the United States was prompted to make its missiles more accurate so that the warheads could still have a decent chance of disabling a Soviet ICBM. (The earlier-generation Minuteman IIs have about the same likelihood of destroying an older Soviet silo as the upgraded Minuteman IIIs have of blowing up a modern, much "harder" silo.)[14]

Current programs continue this pattern, and advance it further. The United States is about to modernize all three components of its Strategic Triad, and make other refinements as well (fine-tuning even more limited "limited options," improving command-control and attack-assessment capabilities, etc.), all in the interests of counterforce. ICBMs are, currently, the best tools for destroying missiles in silos; the other two legs of the Triad are either too inaccurate or too slow to destroy enemy missiles promptly. Therefore, the Carter Administration plans to protect the ICBMs by deploying the new MX mobile missile: several protective shelters will be built for each MX, and the missile can be shuttled around on an elliptical "racetrack" from one shelter to another so the Soviets will never know where the missile actually rests. Theoretically, this will make it much more difficult to destroy all the MX missiles in a first strike.

At the same time, the ICBMs themselves will be made much more lethal. The MX itself is a two-ton monster carrying 10 Mark-12A warheads, each twice as powerful as each of the three warheads on the current Minuteman III, and fitted with a special computer guidance system that will place the warheads within 300 feet of their targets, virtually guaranteeing (in theory) the obliteration of anything a warhead is aimed at.

At the same time, air-launched cruise missiles (ALCMs) —so small that they cannot be tracked by Soviet air-defense radar and so accurate they can (theoretically) destroy anything—will be loaded onto B-52 bombers. ALCMs can be fired from outside Soviet airspace, thus enhancing the survival of the B-52s, which would be getting more and more vulnerable to Soviet air defenses if their mission remained merely penetrating the USSR and dropping bombs. And sometime in the next decade, Trident submarines will probably be fitted with Trident II missiles, each with up to 14 super-accurate warheads, so that the SLBM force, too, will acquire a "hard-target-kill capability" (the Pentagon's euphemism for knocking out missile silos).

In the early 1960s, McNamara and his systems analysts could tell everyone that they were planning according to "assured destruction" guidelines, so that the military needn't bother building all its expensive new counterforce hardware. At the same time, it could still actually plan for limited nuclear war options and counterforce strikes because the Soviets had so few strategic military targets to hit; counterforce attack plans did not really require any more weapons—or any more refined weapons—than the United States already possessed.

However, when the Soviets built more ICBMs, when they began hardening them in silos, and when they made their own weapons more accurate—accurate enough, in theory, to threaten our own ICBM force—U.S. military planners had to make a decision: either change targeting doctrine, de-emphasizing the need for hard-target-killing ICBMs; or change the force to keep up with the doctrinal necessities. The latter option was chosen—or, more to the point, it was pursued, since there never really was any choice about it, at least not in the forum of public debate.

And when James Schlesinger took the helm as Secretary of Defense during the Nixon Administration's second term and brought back some of his old RAND colleagues, who had been deposed when the Republicans first returned to the throne, counterforce came out of the closet.[15] Many arms-controllers panicked, but in fact nothing really changed all that much. It was just that the strategic context—the Soviet build-up—forced the strategy out into the open. At the same time, Schlesinger did initiate refinements in command and control that would make the "limited nuclear options" even more limited, that would create "target packages" smaller and smaller in size and scope, increasingly discriminating in their destructiveness. The "tit-for-tat" game could be played more readily (or so it appeared). In the Carter Administration, Harold Brown extends this strategy even further, under the rubric of a "countervailing strategy," whose name, says Brown, "is newer than the strategy" itself:

It has never been U.S. policy to limit ourselves to massive counter-city operations in retaliation, nor have our plans been so circumscribed. For nearly 20 years, we have explicitly included a range of employment options—against military as well as non-military targets—in our strategic nuclear employment planning . . . In particular, we have always considered it important, in the event of war, to be able to attack the forces that could do damage to the United States and its allies.[16]

Having acquired highly sophisticated technology at relatively low cost, the Defense Department is now emphasizing counterforce and limited options—and doing so publicly. "Assured destruction" is dead; it is no longer viable even as a ruse against the weapons buffs in the services and the research-and-development community. Just as McNamara feared, the high-technology aficionados have taken over the day as more and more sophisticated hardware gets piled onto our five-year defense plans.

Each new advance in U.S. military technology is justified—and widely accepted—not as a continuation and refinement of a strategy that may or may not be wise or bankrupt, but rather as a response to a present or an impending Soviet threat. Such is the rationale—with a vengeance—for the latest generation of nuclear weapons. It is therefore imperative to assess Soviet capabilities, to evaluate the widely held view that the Soviets possess, now or in the very near future, "strategic superiority"—to gauge just what this Soviet threat amounts to, and what the United States should do, if anything, in response. At the same time, it is necessary to assess whether, under the circumstances, continuation of a counterforce-dominant nuclear strategy constitutes the wisest course of action.

II.
THE NEW
AND IMPROVED
SOVIET THREAT!

Renewed fears of Soviet strategic capabilities began to surface in the winter of 1976-77, when the conclusions of "Team B" were leaked to the press. Team B was the *ad hoc* panel chosen by President Ford's Foreign Intelligence Advisory Board to examine whether the CIA was systematically underestimating Soviet military strength. Their answer: Absolutely yes. Largely ignored in the reportage of the Team B hullabaloo was the genesis of the panel. The Ford Administration had deliberately decided to bring in a collection of frankly right-wing Russophobes, headed by Harvard historian Richard Pipes, an expert on pre-revolutionary Russia, just to see if they could take CIA data and come to conclusions quite different from those reached by the in-house analysts. It was an experiment in intelligence analysis, and there was no pretense of objectivity in the selection of Team B members. Yet from the initial press accounts, it appeared that this was just a solid, bipartisan mix of experts who objectively came to some rather frightening conclusions about the Soviets.[1]

At about the same time, the Committee on the Present Danger was formed, with Paul Nitze serving as Policy Director. Nitze was ideal for the job: former Policy Planning Director at State under Dean Acheson, former Secretary of the Navy, former director of International Security Affairs at Defense, former SALT negotiator, a man who had sat on nearly every blue-ribbon panel over the last 25 years that had something hair-raising to say

13

about the impending Soviet threat and the coming years of "maximum danger."[2]

The Team B leak also coincided with the retirement of General George Keegan from the directorate of Air Force Intelligence, consistently the most pessimistic of the intelligence agencies in the U.S. Government. Keegan held press conferences and travelled the speakers' circuit, leaking sensitive intelligence data (but only selectively) and lashing out at the pusillanimity and cowardice that the government was displaying in the face of Soviet military might.[3]

Throughout all this, the Soviets truly were strengthening their forces—no big crash build-up, but undeniably a determined, steady effort to whip their defense posture into something resembling that of a superpower. They began deploying MIRVed ICBMs in a fairly big way, and they improved their missile accuracy. Both actions were quite predictable, but occurred often more quickly than anticipated and were guaranteed to raise enormous fears on the other side of the globe.

Meanwhile, the Pentagon's open-faced counterforce doctrine bloomed. Defense Secretaries Schlesinger, Rumsfeld and Brown all decided to get frank about it. The time, after all, was ripe. With talk of the Soviet threat appearing with increasing frequency in the conversation of officialdom, in Congressional debates, and on the leading editorial pages across the land, talk of blasting away Soviet missile silos and engaging the Russians in "tit-for-tat" games of limited nuclear warfare seemed less provocative and bloodcurdling than it had just a few years ago.

Yet it was the Team B, Nitze and his Maximum Danger squad, and Keegan who attracted the most attention. These men and their many followers base their conclusions on published Soviet doctrine, recent Soviet capabilities and current trends in the U.S.-Soviet military balance. The assumptions on which they base their conclusions, the evidence they muster to support their findings, and their positions generally are the topics of this essay. First, we will take a close look at the allegedly threatening Soviet military literature; then, at allegedly threatening developments in Soviet nuclear weapons procurement; and finally, at what the future brings in new technologies, developments in strategy, and prospects for serious arms control.

Soviet Military Doctrine

The published theoretical writings of several Soviet military officers have alarmed many Western analysts. According to these observers, the writings emphasize nuclear "war-fighting" rather than "war-deterring."

Two things need to be said about these publications. First, such sources are dubious footholds for conclusions as far-reaching as many that have been so unequivocally presented to the public. The published ideas of a particular group of military officers, in *any* country, do not necessarily reflect the actual convictions of the political leaders. Second, a careful reading of many Soviet military sources reveals that some American analysts, such as Pipes, Nitze and others, have seriously misread or distorted their contents.

For example, many U.S. analysts have reported with horror that the Soviets still find the writings of Karl von Clausewitz relevant—Clausewitz, the 19th century philospher-warrior whose masterpiece, *On War,* proclaimed that "war is the continuation of policy by other means." Several cite the late Marshal V.D. Sokolovskiy's statement in his seminal work, *Military Strategy:* "The essential nature of war as a continuation of politics does not change with changing technology and armaments."[4] Some also point out that many Soviet military theorists ridicule—as "idealism" and "metaphysics"—the American notion that nuclear war is fundamentally different from other types of warfare. Some American Sovietologists claim that the Clausewitzian attitudes held by the Russian High Command intrinsically endanger the United States. Professor Pipes goes so far as to contend that "as long as the Soviets persist in adhering to the Clausewitzian maxim on the function of war, mutual deterrence does not really exist."[5]

Such sweeping statements reveal a misunderstanding both of Clausewitz and of Soviet military doctrine. It is true that Marxists who study war tend to be quite taken with Clausewitz. Marx and Engels admired his wisdom

15

Yet nobody . . . has conceived of a credible scenario in which the Soviet leadership would risk a chance of nuclear attack on the Motherland . . .

and keen political perceptions; Lenin filled the margins of his copy of *On War* with annotations and enthusiastic jottings of approval; contemporary Soviet strategists cite him repeatedly, if somewhat simplistically. And true, it was Clausewitz who stressed, among other things, the importance of destroying "the enemy's [armed] power" as the means to attain the object of combat[6]—a sentiment that translates into counterforce in the nuclear age.

However, those who make much of the Clausewitz connection miss his central point:

> Since war is not an act of senseless passion but is controlled by its political object, the value of this object must determine the sacrifices to be made for it in magnitude and also in duration. Once the expenditure of effort exceeds the value of the political object, the object must be renounced and peace must follow.[7]

The authors of one official Soviet document echo this theme: "The scale and intensity of wars are determined first of all by the political aims."[8]

Yet nobody—including those who dwell on Clausewitz and his lineage of contemporary Soviet warplanners—has conceived of a credible scenario in which the Soviet leadership would risk a chance of nuclear attack on the Motherland; no one has thought of a political goal whose gain would be worth the sacrifice of possible American nuclear retaliation. In this sense, the Soviets' resolute political perspective of war should be not frightening, but rather somewhat reassuring.

The perspective found in Soviet military writings, too, is not, in the main, the stuff of nightmares. The connection that the Soviets perceive between war and politics—Clausewitz with a Leninist twist—is summed up in the fifth edition (1972) of *Marxism-Leninism On War & Army,* an official book written by a group of top Soviet

16

military officers and scholars: "Politics will determine when the armed struggle is to be started and what means to be employed. Nuclear war cannot emerge from nowhere, out of a vacuum, by itself . . . " In general,

> war cannot be understood without first understanding its connection with the policies preceding it. . . The political interests of the classes at war and of their conditions determine the war aims, while armed struggle is the means of achieving these aims . . . [W]ar is the continuation of the politics of definite classes and conditions by violent means.[9]

The point is that wars grow out of certain socio-political conflicts, and are the products of certain self-interested policies pursued by certain powers (or, in a Marxist-Leninist framework, classes). There is surely nothing so provocative about all this.

Soviet criticism of American nuclear war doctrine covers similar ground. According to Marxist-Leninist doctrine, modern war is the product of "the aggressive forces of imperialism," i.e., the United States and its allies. Wars, from this viewpoint, are rooted in capitalism, its position as a declining force in the world, and its leaders' desperate attempts to retain unchallenged "world domination." Thus, write the authors of *Marxism-Leninism On War & Army:*

> The bourgeois ideologists do all they can to confuse and distort the question about the sources of wars, their nature, social and class essence . . . By their arguments, the bourgeois theoreticians, consciously or unconsciously, attempt to divorce the nuclear missile war under preparation from the aggressive policies of imperialism . . . [They] conceal who is responsible for imperialist aggression.[10]

Thus, much Soviet criticism of American defense doctrine does not substantively attack notions of deterrence, but rather aims to highlight what the Soviets see as the underlying political foundations of a future nuclear war, and to expose abstract, theoretical discourse on the

17

matter by American technocrats as subterfuge diversions from these fundamental political issues.

Moreover, the historical context of Soviet military writings must be taken into account. Many Soviet articles proclaiming the feasibility of winning a nuclear war were—as pointed out by Harriet Fast Scott, American translator of Sokolovskiy's *magnum opus*—"prompted by Chinese accusations of revisionism."[11] Throughout the late 1950s and early '60s, when many of the first Soviet theoretical documents on nuclear strategy were composed, the Kremlin was continuously under attack from the Maoists for indulging in "revisionism" in its relations with the capitalist camp. At this time, the Sino-Soviet competition for exclusive legitimacy as leaders of the Communist World was an immensely important matter to Soviet leaders, who sought above all else to maintain their control over their geographic sphere of influence and Communist Parties elsewhere.

Comments about winning a nuclear war must also be read in the historical context of post-Khrushchev military affairs. Khrushchev relied almost exclusively on a military strategy of nuclear "minimum deterrence," with the single option of massively retaliating against an attack by the United States. He articulated and implemented this philosophy at the expense, and over the virulent objections, of many military strategists. The succeeding Brezhnev-Kosygin regime stuck with Khrushchev's basic tenets of avoiding general nuclear war and maintaining deterrence; but they agreed with many factions of the military that nuclear war *was* possible (particularly, it could be ideologically justified, so long as imperialism exists) and that, therefore, preparations and contingencies should be developed for meeting this possibility, should it arise. In this sense, Soviet military planning, from 1965 to 1967, underwent a transformation similar to the U.S. Defense Department's transition from "massive retaliation" to "flexible options" in the early 1960s.[12] And the Soviets have, indeed, devoted considerable attention to problems of how to fight a nuclear war, maintaining secure command-and-control, and so forth. However, the temptation to identify a strict dichotomy between "deterrence" and "warfighting," as many American academics do, should be resisted. According to Soviet philosophy, deterrence resides in the ability to fight a war if need be. This view is not so different from that of Harold Brown, as stated in his FY 1981 posture statement:

> There is no contradiction between this attention to the militarily effective targeting of the large and flexible forces we increasingly possess—to how we could fight a war, if need be—and our primary and overriding policy of deterrence.

Indeed, Brown explicitly notes:

> To recognize that strong war-winning views are held in some Soviet circles . . . is not necessarily to cast any accusation of special malevolence, for these are traditional military perspectives by no means unreflected even in current Western discussion of these matters.[13]

Finally, these writings must be seen in the context of Communist ideology. During the late 1960s, an extensive debate was held in the pages of *Voyennaya mysl'* [*Military Thought*] on whether nuclear war would cause the end of civilization. *Military Thought* is circulated confidentially and exclusively within the Soviet military; it is not meant for a civilian or a Western audience; one should not mistake its articles for those in some Soviet publications designed to propagandize the West. The most eloquent and elaborate refutation to the end-of-civilization line was penned by General K. Bochkarev, Deputy Commandant of the General Staff Academy. He stressed that while nuclear war is "unquestionably . . . an adventuristic gamble," still "there is no serious proof that it has already been discarded by the general staffs of the Western powers, and above all by the Pentagon"; that "it is absolutely obvious" that "one cannot take at their face value" denials of aggressiveness by Western military men." Finally, he gets to the real point: that if military strategy and military victory are deemed fictitious in the nuclear age, then

the armed forces of the socialist states . . . will not be

Much evidence suggests that the Soviets seem driven, almost obsessively, often unreasonably, by the idea that the "Western imperialists" might attack the USSR or its socialist allies . . .

able to set for themselves the goal of defeating imperialism and the global nuclear war which it unleashes and the mission of attaining victory in it, and our military science should not even work out a strategy for the conduct of war since the latter has lost its meaning and its significance . . . *In this case, the very call to raise the combat readiness of our armed forces and improve their capability to defeat any aggressor is senseless.*[14]

In short, "The morale-combat qualities of Soviet soldiers are moulded on the basis of the ideology of Marxism-Leninism which . . . instills in them unflagging confidence in the indestructability and final triumph of the forces of socialism."[15] Therefore, if all this talk about no-win scenarios gains much currency, the entire rationale of constant military preparedness and a hefty military build-up will be undermined, as will the role of the Communist Party and the Soviet State as the supreme protector of the people in case of imperialist aggression. In other words, the Soviet military, the Party, and the state all have a stake in insisting that nuclear war is winnable and that socialism can triumph from its ashes.

In fact, however, articles, many of them appearing in *Military Thought*, consider the prospect of nuclear war with no less horror or gravity than do Americans.[16]

The writings of Soviet strategists, taken in their full context, surely do not suggest nuclear warmongering. In fact, much evidence suggests that the Soviets seem driven, almost obsessively, often unreasonably, by the idea that the "Western imperialists" might attack the USSR or its socialist allies; Russia has, after all, been invaded three times in this century. As former CIA Director William Colby testified before the Senate Foreign Relations Committee:

You will find a concern, even a paranoia, over their own security. You will find the determination that they shall never again be invaded and put through the kinds of turmoil that they have been under many different invasions ... I think that they ... want to overprotect themselves to make certain that that does not happen, and they are less concerned about the image that that presents to their neighbors, thinking that their motives are really defensive and pure and therefore other people should not be suspicious of them.[17]

In fact, the Soviet view of the interrelationship between war and politics is integrally linked with the fear of a possible attack. In a critique of Soviet columnist Aleksandr Bovin, who argued that nuclear war cannot serve as a political instrument, Soviet Col. Ye. Rybkin wrote:

While correctly asserting that a total nuclear war is not acceptable as a means of achieving a political goal, A. Bovin at the same time makes a noticeable methodological mistake ... [N]either the nature of the modern era nor nuclear weapons have changed the position that *nuclear war, if the imperialists were able to unleash one, would be an extension of policy.* Those individuals who deny this are confusing the causes, essence, and social nature of the phenomenon with the expediency of using it as a means of achieving a political goal.

So long as there exist the economic bases for wars and a policy which is capable of generating a war, we cannot abandon a class evaluation of the functions of such a war, even though it exists only as a possibility. The great threat of a nuclear war on the part of antisocialist, primarily anti-Soviet, forces is an extension of reactionary imperialist policy and a war would be an extension of this policy, if a nuclear conflict were to break out ... *From this point of view,* no principle changes in the interrelationship between war and policy have occurred.[18]

At the same time, Rybkin quotes the Communist

Party of the Soviet Union as declaring that an all-out nuclear war "cannot and must not serve as a means of solving international disputes."[19]

Thus, if Richard Pipes and others are correct in insisting that we should take Soviet military writings seriously, Rybkin's article—and much of Sokolovskiy and what is published in confidential journals such as *Military Thought*—seem to suggest that the Soviets will *not* use nuclear weapons for political gain, but that they suspect the United States might and that therefore the Soviet camp must be prepared to make the best of things if war does erupt.

Some American analysts insist, nevertheless, that the Soviets would not mind suffering a retaliatory blow delivered by the United States if they could accomplish vast political gains (though they never specify what these might be) in the process. T.K. Jones—Paul Nitze's private systems analyst—has asserted in Congressional testimony, "I firmly believe that the present Soviet leadership would have no qualms in risking the loss of 20 million or so of its population . . . "[20] Richard Pipes reckons that they would probably not mind losing 30 million; after all, they lost a similar percentage of their population during World War II.[21] Leaving aside for a moment the fact that 20 or 30 million certainly underestimates Soviet losses in a nuclear war, several points must be made here.

First, the Soviets did not enter World War II knowing that 20 million Russians would die in battle. Second, the deaths and all the assorted injuries were spread out over four years, not thirty minutes or so, as would be the case in a nuclear catastrophe. Third, the Soviet decision to go to war was an act of self-defense in the face of impending Nazi conquest—not, as would be the case in the launching or provocation of nuclear war, a display of suicidal adventurism. Fourth, the Soviets were able to save much of their industrial base by transporting it eastward by rail as the Nazis started plowing through Russian territory from the west; in a nuclear war, for which there would be little warning and during which targets all across the country could be blasted, they would have no such assurances in advance.

Still, according to some hardliners, a nuclear war

might not be so devastating. After all, some trains in Hiroshima were running 48 hours after the blast; many buildings were left standing; and—as Professor Pipes cites British physicist P.M.S. Blackett's observation in the latter's 1949 book, *Fear, War and the Bomb*— Germany was hit with the blast equivalent of 400 Hiroshimas in the course of World War II and was still able to fight.[22] This is all highly misleading. First, Blackett changed his views on the military implications of nuclear weaponry after the first successful explosion of the hydrogen bomb, which proved that explosive yields of weapons could be theoretically limitless. Second, comparing nuclear with conventional blasts ignores the effects of radiation, fallout, thermal heat, electromagnetic pulse and other effects of nuclear weapons.[23] Third, the Hiroshima bomb was 14 kilotons, the equivalent of a 14,000-ton dynamite blast. About one-third of Hiroshima was directly hit. The smallest weapon in the U.S. strategic arsenal today is the Poseidon with 40 kilotons. And just one-sixth of the U.S. nuclear-missile submarine force alone—seven or eight subs, each loaded with 160 nuclear warheads—could thoroughly devastate all 220 Soviet cities with populations greater than 100,000.[24]

At the 30th Anniversary Celebration of the Great Patriotic War Victory, otherwise an occasion for Soviet self-glorification, Leonid Brezhnev declared that "the starting of a nuclear missile war would spell inevitable annihilation for the aggressor himself, to say nothing of the vast losses for many other countries perhaps not even formally involved in the war."[25] The same sentiment is expressed by various authors writing in *Military Thought,* by Marshal Sokolovskiy, by the authors of *Marxism-Leninism On War & Army.* Furthermore, in the first business meeting of the two SALT delegations in Helsinki, on November 18, 1969, the Soviet Delegation, in a little-known prepared statement, cleared by the highest political and military leaders, noted:

Even in the event that one of the sides were the first to be subjected to attack, it would undoubtedly retain the ability to inflict a retaliatory strike of crushing power. Thus, evidently, we all agree that war between our two

23

The Soviets seem just as horrified about the prospects and consequences of nuclear war as anybody.

countries would be disastrous for both sides. And it would be tantamount to suicide for the ones who decided to start such a war.[26]

A closer look at much of Soviet military literature, in short, reveals a picture quite different from that which Professor Pipes and and others paint. The Soviets have obviously been influenced by Clausewitz; but this means only that they see the nature and intensity of war as being determined by political factors, and since nobody has figured out any political goal for which the Soviets might be willing to risk nuclear holocaust, the Clausewitz connection can hardly be seen as horrifying or as inimical to the prospects of deterrence. Soviet military literature does emphasize what happens after nuclear war begins more than American literature does; but this concern seems to grow out of a genuine fear of an attack on the Soviet Union by the United States or its allies; this fear has historical basis. In any event, the Soviets have not apparently worked out a decent operational definition of "winning" a nuclear war, or how to get there from here. Finally, the Soviets seem just as horrified about the prospects and consequences of nuclear war as anybody.

In short, very little in Soviet military doctrine lends credence to the proposition that, in Richard Pipes' words, "the Soviet Union thinks it can fight and win a nuclear war."

Soviet Military Capabilities

Doctrine, of course, is one thing; action, quite another. Many Western analysts see trends in Soviet military developments that support their thesis that the Soviets are acquiring "strategic superiority." These analyses often point to various indices of this superiority: (1) rising military expenditures, especially for investment in strategic arms; (2) numerical superiority in missiles; (3)

24

development of "heavy missiles," high in both throw-weight and megatonnage; (4) extensive civil defense planning; (5) new anti-ballistic missile developments, especially in charged-particle-beam technology; and (6) deployment of large numbers of highly accurate warheads, theoretically capable of knocking out 90 percent of American land-based missiles by the early-to-mid 1980s. But what do all these things say, and what do they mean?

1. Military Expenditures

There is no question that the Soviets spend more money on defense—and more money on strategic nuclear forces—than does the United States; there is some question, however, as to how significant this distinction actually is.

For example, the CIA estimates that last year the USSR spent about 50 percent more on defense than did the United States, when calculated in dollars.[27] There are serious flaws, however, in the way the Soviet budget is estimated by U.S. intelligence agencies, flaws freely admitted by the CIA. "Estimated dollar costs," says one recent CIA report on Soviet military expenditures, "do not measure actual Soviet defense expenditures or their burden on the Soviet economy."[28] This is because the CIA examines the Soviet military machine and calculates what the United States would have to pay for the same troops, weapons, research and development, and so forth. Although the Russians draft their soldiers and pay them about four rubles a week, the CIA figures their wage bill by asking how much they would be paid in American all-volunteer Army wages. So, when the U.S. military switched to higher pay-scales, and when American inflation significantly increased, the Soviet defense budget also appeared to "rise" considerably.[29]

The CIA also compares the U.S. and Soviet defense budgets in terms of Russian rubles—a much fairer way of measuring the Soviet effort—and the Soviets still end up outspending the United States, but by much less, about 25 percent.[30] It's the best the CIA can do, perhaps, but inadequacies are inevitable here, too. The Soviet Union is a command economy; there is no market as we know it. As a RAND Corporation study notes, "It is well known that the administered nature of Soviet prices makes them deficient tools for analysis of real costs."[31]

Even accepting the 25 percent superiority, the figure must be probed more closely. The CIA has estimated that the Soviets spend about 35 percent of their defense rubles to cover the Chinese border,[32] whereas nearly all of the American defense effort focuses somehow around the various borders of the USSR or its Warsaw Pact allies. Thus, excluding China, American and Soviet spending is roughly equal, when compared in rubles.

Looking at strategic nuclear forces only, the Soviets are believed to outspend the United States by two-and-a-half times.[33] A closer look, however, reveals that this doesn't mean much, either. Only about 40 percent of the Soviet strategic budget actually goes to "intercontinental attack" (ICBMs, SLBMs, heavy bombers and their support and communication equipment). The rest goes mostly to "peripheral nuclear weapons," missiles aimed at Western Europe and China.[34] While these arms are of obvious concern to the United States, they are generally not considered a part of the *strategic* balance. At the same time, the United States spends about 60 percent of its strategic-force budget on weapons for intercontinental attack.[35] Thus, looking at intercontinental-attack forces alone, the Soviets outspend the United States (in dollars) by one-and-a-half, not two-and-a-half, times.[36]

That still seems a hefty margin, and the Soviets have, no doubt, been buying a great deal. Just the past five years, they have deployed three new ICBMs (SS-17, SS-18, SS-19), two new SLBMs (SS-N-8 and SS-N-18), and are developing a new generation of ICBMs, some more SLBMs, a new nuclear-missile submarine and, some reports say, a new heavy bomber. They also spend a lot of money on command-and-control security, and have been experimenting in such exotica as anti-satellite weapons, laser beams and so forth—items of dubious utility, but very costly nevertheless.

The question must be asked: What are the Soviets getting for all their money? If they are spending 50 percent more than the United States, are they getting 50 percent more capability?

There is no strict relationship between money and effectiveness in strategic weapons—or, for that matter, in anything. Recently, for instance, the United States modified the computer guidance systems in all 550 of its Minuteman III ICBMs, doubling each missile's accuracy (from 1200 to 600 feet average-miss) and thereby tripling its ability to destroy Soviet missile silos (from 19 to 55 percent on a single shot). The cost of this improvement: a mere $155 million.[37] The Soviets, meanwhile, accomplished the same improvement, but they did it by purchasing four entirely new missiles and deploying three of them. Their estimated cost: $28.5 billion.[38] The Soviets *did* get more warheads out of their improvement, and are thus able to hit more targets with them, but the U.S. improvement was nearly five times more cost-effective than that of the Soviets.[39]

Clearly, one must examine not only how much money is being spent, but what is being bought with it. The intervening variable here is efficiency—and in strategic nuclear weapons, anyway, America is far more efficient. The United States modifies existing systems to get improvements; the USSR, every few years, perhaps due to pressures inside the weapon design bureaus, cranks out a whole new missile. Having mastered microminiaturization of highly sophisticated electronic gear at relatively low cost, the United States can improve the accuracy of its missile warheads, introduce retargeting features and other fancy footwork, in a fairly small amount of space and fairly cheaply; the Soviets require big computers and lots of mass to do the same thing, and it ends up costing a lot more.

In short, tallying dollars doesn't tell much about the effectiveness of nuclear weapons—much less about the state of the strategic balance. The Soviets are doing more, and they have become a formidable military power; but their methods are far more inefficient than ours; they get far less "bang for the buck" (or "rubble for the ruble"). Therefore, comparing military spending—in dollars *or* in rubles—does not bring us anywhere close to the essence of the military balance.

2. Missiles and Bombers

A familiar charge hurled by those who warn of impending (or present) danger is that the Soviet Union has more *strategic delivery vehicles*—missile launchers and heavy bombers—than the United States. True, the USSR has 1,398 ICBM launchers, while the United States has 1,054; they have 947 submarine-launched missile tubes, while the U.S. has 656; and they have 156 heavy bombers, while we have 348. (Most of these tallies conveniently omit bombers.) All in all, the USSR has 2,501 delivery vehicles, while the United States has 2,124.[40]

The number of missiles meant something in the days before multiple independently targetable warheads. Now that figure, at least as an indicator of offensive strength, has very limited utility. More relevant is the number of warheads and bombs. The U.S. strategic nuclear arsenal contains more than 9,400 weapons, while the Soviets have about 6,000.[41] Moreover, fifty-five percent of U.S. nuclear-missile submarines are on station—ready to fire—at any given moment, whereas only fifteen percent of Soviet subs are so poised; and one third of American bombers are on constant runway alert, while no Soviet bombers are.[42] U.S. missiles are also considered, in general, more reliable and more accurate than Soviet weapons.

A warhead count has its limits as well. The number of weapons must be considered in light of what these weapons are supposed to do and what they are able to do. Just about any warhead of adequate range and reliability can knock out some section of a city. But it takes special features to destroy targets that are hardened to resist strong blast, such as missile silos. If a nation's strategy involves the destruction of these sorts of targets, then more than the mere number of warheads must be looked into. In any event, it can be stated with certainty that just counting the number of missile launchers does not get us close to anything meaningful.

3. "Heavy Missiles": Throw-Weight and Megatonnage

The most common measure used by those seeking some qualitative index of the strategic balance—something

Comparing Soviet and American throw-weight and hoping to derive any conclusions from such a comparison can only be, at best, misleading and, at worst, dishonest.

beyond numbers of launchers and warheads—is *throw-weight*. Throw-weight is simply the gross weight of the top stage of a missile—its warheads, guidance systems, the re-entry vehicle (RV) that holds these things and the "post-boost vehicle" encasing them all.

This measure has become the magic key for those eager to prove that the Soviets are way ahead of the United States in the strategic arms race. Some of these people refer to throw-weight as the single best indicator of an arsenal's ability to destroy hardened targets, such as missile silos; others see it as the best indicator of the amount of territory a missile can demolish.[43]

In fact, throw-weight is not very good for either of those things, or for much of anything generally. One notable example of its general irrelevance:

This year, the United States will begin to install Mark-12A warheads on 300 of its Minuteman III missiles. The replacement of the old Mark-12s with the Mark-12A will add a mere 35 pounds to the 2000-lb. throw-weight of the missile. Yet the new warhead releases twice as much destructive power as the old warheads—335 kilotons, versus 170.[44] That is, the United States will get twice the blast with a mere 2 percent boost in throw-weight.

Another example: The Soviet's SS-18 ICBM has twice as much throw-weight as the planned U.S. MX ICBM will have—16,000, as compared with just under 8000 pounds. Yet both missiles will hold 10 warheads (and both could hold, without any alteration in yield, four more); and while the SS-18's explosive yield is somewhat higher than that of the MX, the MX will have a higher chance of destroying missile silos because of its superior accuracy.[45]

In short, throw-weight tells little about a warhead's capacity to destroy area or hard targets. True, if you take a missile and add more throw-weight, then you could put

29

more or heavier warheads on that missile. But comparing Soviet and American throw-weight and hoping to derive any conclusions from such a comparison can only be, at best, misleading and, at worst, dishonest.

It's dishonest because in the mid-1960s the Defense Department made a conscious and deliberate choice to trade in throw-weight for accuracy. The new strategy of the McNamara regime emphasized flexible options rather than simply massive retaliation. This meant destroying particular military or industrial facilities, rather than whole cities. In response, the defense laboratories developed warheads that were more accurate and that could, consequently, deliver the same probability of damage with lower explosive yields. They devised calculations showing that improved accuracy meant that gigantic missiles were unnecessary.

Throw-weight comparisons are dishonest, in other words, because the United States doesn't need heavy throw-weight to perform its strategic missions. Of all the people who complain about the Soviet SS-18, the only "heavy" missile in either superpower's arsenal, nobody proposes that the United States should, or needs to, build anything so huge. Everyone recognizes that it simply isn't needed.

Second, technological exigencies compel the Soviets to make their missiles heavier than those in the U.S. arsenal. Soviet technicians have not perfected the microminiaturization of computers and electronic circuitry for high-performance inertial guidance systems; and, for the same reason that developing such a capability is more expensive—compared to what it costs the United States to do the same thing—it also involves heavier fuzing devices, guidance systems, and other electronic gear, often two or three times heavier than comparable systems in U.S. missiles.[46] That is, per kiloton of explosive yield, the Soviets require more pounds of throw-weight than do the Americans.

All in all, then, throw-weight is, at best, an imprecise and, at worst, a highly misleading indicator of strategic strength. Comparisons based on throw-weight should not be seen as reflecting the strategic balance.

30   Some analysts point to *explosive yield* as an index of

the balance. Certainly this is much more direct than throw-weight. It does reflect more accurately the damage each side can wreak upon the other. But it too is an inadequate measure.

First, contrary to intuition, the scope of a weapon's destructive power is not proportional to its explosive yield. After all, when a bomb explodes, its effects burst in three dimensions, whereas the earth's surface has only two. Thus, as yield increases, the area of damage expands by the two-thirds power of yield (or, if the weapon exceeds one megaton, the square root of yield). In other words, while ten one-megaton bombs equal ten "equivalent megatons," one ten-megaton bomb equals only 3.16 equivalent megatons (or EMT).

Since the Soviets have fewer and larger warheads than the U.S., not adjusting megatonnage to account for this factor seriously distorts any comparison of military strength between the two superpowers.

Comparisons based on EMT, while more useful, have little relevance, as well. Equivalent megatonnage is a measure of *area* damage; for a mutual-assured-destruction or "city-busting" strategy, it is a perfect measure. However, as noted earlier, neither the United States nor the USSR aim to destroy whole cities—or any other sort of "area" target—in their nuclear targeting plans. Rather, they aim to destroy particular "point" targets. All things equal, high-yield weapons have a better chance of destroying particular targets than lower-yield weapons. However, nuclear warheads are becoming so accurate that yield or equivalent megatonnage has increasingly diminished impact.*

*In the trade-off between yield and accuracy, increments in accuracy-improvement provide far more lethality than comparable improvements in yield. This is dramatically illustrated in a formula known as the "lethality factor" (or "K"):

$$K = \frac{Y^{2/3}}{(CEP)^2}$$

where Y=yield of the weapon, in megatons; and CEP=circular error probable, or the distance within which a warhead is likely to land from the intended target 50 percent of the time. This translates to mean that doubling the accuracy boosts "K" as much as boosting yield by eight times. Once a warhead becomes so accurate that it lands inside the crater made by the explosion, then yield becomes manifestly insignificant.

The lesson here is to beware of analyses that focus on "static indicators"— simple bean-counts, step-on-the-scales comparisons, or anything of the sort.

In short, EMT sheds no light on either side's ability to execute its strategic plans. And questions of the strategic balance have little meaning unless they convey something about each side's ability to perform its military mission, whatever that mission might be.

The lesson here is to beware of analyses that focus on "static indicators"—simple bean-counts, step-on-the-scales comparisons, or anything of the sort. The important questions, the only really relevant questions, are: What is the purpose of nuclear weapons? What constitutes deterrence? And, under pessimistic circumstances, is Country A or B able to carry out its designed mission? If the answer is "Yes," then there is a balance; if the answer is "No," then there is not.

Here is where analyses of the Soviet threat come in. If the Soviets are building toward "strategic superiority," that does not mean merely that they have more megatonnage or throw-weight or whatever than the United States does. As we have seen, these static indicators prove nothing by themselves. If "strategic superiority" means anything, it means that they are developing the capacity to prevent the United States from performing its strategic missions; if the United States cannot do that, then perhaps it cannot deter the Soviets from nuclear adventurism or from posing unanswerable nuclear threats for political gain.

Acquiring "superiority," in this sense, requires a lot. The scribes of the Soviet threat claim, of course, that the Soviets are definitely on their way. They argue that the USSR is "neutralizing" the U.S. deterrent force in three broad ways: first, by developing a massive and well-coordinated civil defense program—preparing plans to evacuate cities and to reinforce and disperse industry, in other words, to "deny" its targets to U.S. weapons; second, by developing new technologies to shoot down American missiles before they reach Soviet territory; and third, by offensively aiming its warheads at U.S. strategic forces and developing the capability to destroy so many of them that a U.S. retaliation to a Soviet pre-emptive strike will be so feeble as to be useless or counter-productive. Let us look at all three allegations in turn.

4. Soviet Civil Defense

A very big scare was raised a few years ago, and then again in 1978, over the specter of Soviet civil defense.[47] The fever seems to have cooled off a bit since then, but these things move in cycles, and it is a safe bet that the issue will return again in full force. Even now, newspaper and journal articles continue to comment casually on the Soviets' enormous civil defense program and its devastating consequences for the future of deterrence.

The chief doomsayers on this issue include Professor Leon Goure of the University of Miami's Center for Advanced International Studies, who has been writing somber tomes and pamphlets about Soviet civil defense for more than 20 years; General George Keegan, retired Director of Air Force Intelligence; and T.K. Jones, a consultant for Boeing Aerospace and systems-analyst for Paul Nitze.[48] These three and several others proclaim that because of highly developed evacuation and industrial-protection plans, the Soviets could survive a retaliatory nuclear strike from the U.S. and end up with *only* 2 to 10 percent of its population dead—that's 5 to 25 million people—and with full industrial recovery feasible within two to four years after the blast. This, they say, destroys mutual deterrence. Retired General Daniel O. Graham, former Director of the Defense Intelligence Agency (DIA), spells out the nightmare plot:

> The Soviets evacuate their cities and hunker down. Then they move against NATO or Yugoslavia or China or the Middle East with superior conventional forces. The United States is faced with the demand to stay out or risk nuclear exchange in which 100 million Americans would die, as opposed to 10 million Russians.[49]

Where do General Graham and all these serious-minded   33

professionals get these ideas? Mostly from Soviet civil defense manuals. But manuals do not necessarily reflect reality.

For example, the Soviets have never staged an evacuation drill in any major city, nor have they completely emptied even a small town.[50] CIA Director Stansfield Turner sees "little evidence today of serious efforts at mass indoctrination of the population" on civil defense.[51] Even Leon Goure admits that the apathy of the population poses a real problem to the success of the program.[52] In Russian, "civil defense" is translated as *grazhdanskaya oborona.* Taking the first two letters of each word, many Russians skeptically refer to civil defense as *grob,* meaning "coffin."[53]

These shortcomings are apparently evident to Soviet leaders. USSR Civil Defense Chief, Marshal Aleksandr Altunin, complains that high-level civil defense training has taken place

> after a delay, and at times at a low methodological level. Many people assembled for such sessions and were led through the various points of a demonstration exercise, but the trainees did not receive what was most necessary. The practical portion was poorly organized and in a stereotyped manner.[54]

The Party and Politburo leaders are also aware of bureaucratic indifference to civil defense programs, of the Russian talent to avoid unpleasant tasks or sacrifice free time, of the avoidance of the program altogether by many professionals who travel, of the many factory managers who deliberately schedule command-staff exercises during the busiest work periods so that the drills have to be cancelled, and so forth.[55]

An evacuation would be messy. Roads in the Soviet Union are poor and transportation is quite limited. Calculations show that at least 20 million of those who would evacuate the cities must walk—and this figure optimistically assumes masterful coordination and full accessibility of existing motor and rail transport, all without a single prior rehearsal.[56] These poor souls are to walk for a day, then build "expedient shelters." There is

34

no sign that the materials needed for these shelters—Professor Goure lists what he calls the "handy" materials as timber, boards, sheet-metal, bricks, cinder-blocks and shovels[57]—exist in large numbers or are properly distributed. With an evacuation lacking shelters, at least 70 million would die, according to the optimistic estimate of T.K. Jones.[58] Since hospitals, houses, factories, food-processing centers and so forth would be wiped out in the cities, millions more would die later, especially if it were winter.[59]

The industrial base of the economy would be wrecked. Soviet manuals mention means of hardening industry, but even T.K. Jones admits

The extent to which the Soviets have implemented such measures is not known; neither do we know of the specifics of the construction techniques referred to ... [D]escriptions are not sufficiently explicit to estimate the practicality and effectiveness of protective measures for industrial machinery.[60]

An extensive CIA analysis goes farther: "Little evidence exists that would suggest a comprehensive program for hardening economic installations . . . Overall, the measures the Soviets have taken to protect their economy would not prevent massive damage from an attack designed to destroy Soviet economic facilities."[61] Many industries simply *cannot* be protected, among them the USSR's most crucial—oil refineries, power plants, chemical storage facilities, steelmaking works, truck and tractor plants, repair and spare parts facilities, and so forth.[62]

Jones and others refer to the "dispersion" of Soviet industry, suggesting that because the economic resources of the country have been spread so thinly among so many targets, America's surviving warheads would not destroy a very high percentage of the industrial base. This is all mythology. True, there have been orders to disperse industry, and there are laws placing limits on how many people can live in big cities—all with little if any consequence. Some dispersal has taken place, most of it east of the Urals. However, this trend is borne of economic

Virtually every sector of the Soviet economy is highly centralized, and the great bulk of its productive capacity lies in the large urban centers. In short, it wouldn't take very many warheads to do devastating damage to the Soviet industrial structure.

necessity, not military strategy. The USSR's western regions are undergoing substantial depletion of vital resources. Naturally, therefore, Soviet economic planners are spending massive sums of money exploiting the resources of Siberia and transporting them westward.[63]

At the same time, however, new and very large industrial and power plants continue to be constructed in the major cities. And new machinery continues to be installed in existing plants. The latest Five Year Plan allocates more than two-thirds of its capital investment for modernization of existing plants. The Plan explicitly curtails the growth of new construction in favor of renovation. And the construction patterns for many industries are becoming not more dispersed, but increasingly dense.[64] Since World War II—and no less true today than 30 years ago—Soviet economic leaders have stressed concentration, specialization and centralization.[65]

Statistics tell the story. Almost all the chemical plants in the USSR sit in 25 cities. Sixty percent of all natural steel is produced in 25 plants. The entire Central and Volga regions, with 59 million people, receive most of their electricity from five power-plants. There are only 34 major petroleum refineries, eight copper refineries, four plants are located in five cities. There are only six turbine generator works, three of them in Leningrad, another in Kharkov. Almost all engineering work is done in seven cities. Almost all transmission equipment for Siberian powerplants is manufactured in Leningrad, Moscow, Kharkov and Riga. There are only eight major shipbuilding works, 16 major heavy-machine and 15 major agricultural machine-producing plants. The list can go on and on.[66]

According to a study by the U.S. Office of Technology Assessment, three Minuteman III ICBMs (9 warheads) and seven Poseidon SLBMs (63 warheads) could destroy 73 percent of Soviet industrial refining capacity.[67] And a study by the U.S. Arms Control and Disarmament Agency estimates that 150 plants hold 50 percent of the Soviet capacity to produce primary metals, chemicals, petroleum construction equipment, agricultural and railroad equipment, synthetic rubber and power generators. Only 400 plants—that is, 400 targets—produce 75 percent of this output.[68]

Virtually every sector of the Soviet economy is highly centralized, and the great bulk of its productive capacity lies in the large urban centers. In short, it wouldn't take very many warheads to do devastating damage to the Soviet industrial structure. The Soviet economy—deliberately concentrated to make most efficient use of a heavily bottlenecked and centralized planning system—is not at all conducive to a civil defense program designed to survive an all-out retaliatory attack by the United States.

Even if the Russian people and government were enthusiastic about civil defense, even if the Soviet economy could absorb such an effort and still come out alive, T.K. Jones provides a figure that would surely give any Soviet leader pause before evacuating his cities as prelude to an attack on the United States. Jones notes that after a first strike by the USSR, the United States would have only half of its submarines remaining (why he assumes there would be *no* bombers or ICBMs, he doesn't say). With such an arsenal, he says, the United States could, at most, destroy three percent of Soviet territory. However, he also notes that "the top 200 cities total about one-fourth of one percent of Soviet land area."[69] If Jones' figures are correct, that means that we could blast every one of these cities twelve times over, or destroy them only a few times and still have warheads left over for other targets.

In sum, even the most aggressive of Soviet adventurists could not possibly find any rationale for launching, or threatening to launch, a nuclear first strike with any expectation that their civil defense program would more than marginally protect the Russian Motherland, its people, its military structure, and its industry—in short, the source of strength it would need for carrying out and sustaining the sorts of military threats for which, according to Goure, Jones and others, the Soviets established a civil defense program to begin with.*

5. Charged-Particle-Beam Weapons

Another way to "neutralize" the American retaliatory force is to shoot it down with anti-ballistic-missile (ABM) weapons. For quite some time, both sides had actively deployed missiles for this purpose, but they had numerous technical problems and were finally restricted by the ABM Treaty of 1972. (Research and development efforts were not banned, however, and both sides pursue them vigorously.)

Two years ago, retired Air Force Intelligence Chief General George Keegan, Jr., revealed to the trade journal *Aviation Week and Space Technology* that the USSR was developing the ultimate ABM device—"a "charged-particle-beam" weapon that could wipe out the entire U.S. missile force by the early 1980s. With such a system in place, the Soviets could execute a first strike attack or threaten to do so, knowing that, when the United States retaliates, the Soviets could destroy most or all of the incoming American warheads with a high-speed electronically charged beam; or, if the beam mechanism were deployed on a satellite in outer space, it could destroy U.S. missiles in the middle of their trajectories before they have even unloaded their warheads.[70] If this were true, deterrence would be wrecked, for the United States would have nothing with which to retaliate in the event of a Soviet first strike.

It is true that the Soviets are doing research on military applications of charged-particle physics. The United States has long been working on such technologies as well, and has just recently stepped up its efforts

---

*A much fuller treatment of the Soviet civil defense issue can be found in Fred M. Kaplan, "The Soviet Civil Defense Myth," *Bulletin of the Atomic Scientists,* March and April 1978; Fred M. Kaplan, "Soviet Civil Defense: Some Myths in the Western Debate," *Survival,* May-June 1978.

along these lines. Several experts who are familiar with R&D programs on both sides report that these efforts have proved, and will likely keep proving, fruitless. There is a big difference between researching a project and developing it, a bigger difference between that and incorporating it into a weapon system, and a greater one still between that and operating it effectively. One well-placed defense consultant who is technically expert on these matters remarks: "To say that the Soviets are working on particle beams and to infer from that the sort of thing that Keegan suggests, is like observing that the Soviets are working on a new kind of thread, and concluding that they will price the French clothing industry out of the market within a decade."

A charged-particle-beam system, according to weapons specialist Richard Garwin and others, would have to include long-range sensors to detect and track incoming warheads (or boosted missiles), would have to discriminate against decoys, generate a charged-particle beam, point and track that beam and propagate it through the atmosphere without dissipation while avoiding the earth's magnetic field (which would probably bend the beam), detect and measure near misses, correct for them, and aim again. And it would have to do all this against hundreds or thousands of warheads whooshing down at speeds of five miles per second. If beamed from a satellite in outer space, the system would need incredible amounts of energy continuously (several large power-plants' worth), and its orbit would have to be perfectly synchronized to be in the right place at the right time when the missiles were launched from earth. Such positioning would be relatively easy against ICBMs, whose launch positions are known in advance, but very difficult against SLBMs, which could be launched from any number of underseas positions.[71] Physicists John Parmentola and Kosta Tsipis estimate that the Soviets would need 150 beam-platforms in outer space to get full coverage of possible American launch points.[72]

Even if all this could be handled, the U.S. could develop fairly cheap countermeasures that would effectively nullify the Soviets' efforts. We could destroy the charged-particle-beam satellite with very light explosives; we could jam the link between the weapon and ground control; our missiles or warheads could shoot out "chaff" (thin aluminum shreddings or other materials which show up on radar), to trick and confuse the weapon's sensors; we could even shoot out a thin layer of air from the missile to disperse the beam just before it hit.[73]

In short, a charged-particle-beam ABM would be even more complicated and infeasible than the ABM missile systems that both sides abandoned in 1972—not least because the beam would have to hit the missile or warhead dead-center. Defense Secretary Harold Brown, a trained physicist, tends to discount all claims that the Soviets are effectively developing such a system. "The laws of physics," he notes, "are the same in the United States and the Soviet Union."[74]

6. ICBM Vulnerability

Over the past two years, the issue of "Minuteman vulnerability"—once the most esoteric of theoretical concerns—has dominated discussion of the strategic balance, SALT, and the future of the American nuclear arsenal. It is the chief concern of today's more eminent strategic pessimists; it worries everyone from Senators to network news commentators; and it is the subject of the most nightmarish of scenarios in an analytic dreamworld already overflowing with terror and morbidity.

The scenario generally goes something like this:

By the early to mid-1980s, the Soviets will have acquired enough ICBM warheads of sufficient accuracy to destroy about 90 percent of America's 1000 Minuteman ICBMs (the 54 Titan IIs, sheltered in much lighter silos, are pretty easy to pick off today). Once our ICBMs are mostly gone, the scenario continues, our remaining forces can strike only Soviet cities; however, if we do so, the Soviets would respond by annihilating American cities with their large reserve forces; thus, we don't do anything; our deterrent is deterred; we lose the war; the Soviets "Finlandize" or dominate the free world. (A variation has it that the Soviets don't actually strike first; but everybody knows how this nuclear chessgame would be

*"Strategic analysis is a dream world.
It is the realm of data-free analysis.
There's no test data, no combat data."
Everything we know about the results
of a Soviet first strike comes exclusively
from rather abstract calculations.*

played out, so all the Soviets have to do is threaten to launch the first strike, and we would surrender, knowing how the endgame would be resolved.)[75]

This is a truly scary scenario. But everything about it is wrong—from initial assumptions, to operational calculations, to final conclusions. Three questions must be posed in pursuing this matter. First, are the Minuteman missiles *really* vulnerable (or just theoretically vulnerable)? Second, if they are, does it make much difference? Third, if they are, and if it does matter, what should we do about it?

Are the Minutemen Really Vulnerable?

As defense analyst Pierre Sprey says, "Strategic analysis is a dream world. It is the realm of data-free analysis. There's no test data, no combat data."[76] Everything we know about the results of a Soviet first strike comes exclusively from rather abstract calculations. The RAND Corporation, GE-Tempo, the Defense Department and others issue various types of "bomb-damage calculators," circular slide-rules that do neat little tricks without which the doomsayers would be nowhere. Assume the yield of a weapon, its accuracy and the "hardness" (blast-resistance, formulated in terms of pounds-per-square-inch overpressure) of the target; spin the plastic wheels of the bomb-damage calculator until the arrows line up with those numbers; look at the appropriate window; and presto!, there's the "kill-probability." Then, take out a simple pocket calculator, estimate the kill-probability of *two* warheads exploding on that target, multiply by some arbitrary reliability rate, and you have the overall kill-probability. If the kill-probability is 0.9, extrapolate that to 2000 warheads fired against

41

1000 Minuteman silos, and we conclude that the Soviets can destroy 90 percent of Minutemen.[77]

Anyone who knows the difference between a piece of paper and the real world must realize that this methodology has certain limitations. As an Office of Technology Assessment (OTA) study points out, "The effects of a nuclear war that cannot be calculated are at least as important as those for which calculations are attempted."[78] The OTA was referring to the physical effects of nuclear war on people, industry and the atmosphere; but the same principle applies, plus some, to effects on missile silos.

Massive uncertainties face a nuclear aggressor. Destruction of missile silos depends crucially on the accuracy of the missile warhead, calculated as its CEP—circular-error-probable, or the distance from the target within which a warhead is likely to land *50 percent of the time.* Yet in a nuclear attack, the "cosmic dice" are rolled only once, and who knows how the probabilities will turn out? For example, a one-megaton warhead with a 600-foot CEP has a 92 percent chance of destroying a Minuteman III missile silo (assuming perfect reliability). If, however, in actual performance the CEP were actually 720 feet—a mere 20 percent degradation—the warhead would have only an 83 percent chance; and 280, rather than 132, Minuteman III warheads would probably survive.

Moreover, accuracy will *inevitably* degrade in performance, and sometimes by more than 20 percent. Accuracy depends not merely on the computer guidance systems inside the missile, but also on the range and reentry angle. Further, on a MIRVed missile, the second warhead fired will tend to be somewhat less accurate than the first, the third less accurate than the second, and so forth. There is no single CEP for a particular type of missile; the CEP is the average of the CEPs of the various warheads—which are, themselves, averages—depending on the precise re-entry angle and the warhead's position on the MIRV container (or "bus").[79]

In short, if a warhead has a 0.9 kill-probability, one cannot truly infer that 90 percent of the American ICBMs targeted will be destroyed. It only means that those warheads will have, on average, a 90 percent chance of destroying their targets, but that some of them will have (on average) less than a 90 percent chance and some (on average) more. The chance of a substantial error in accuracy—and the actual degree of such errors—is, therefore, much greater than most analysts acknowledge or, perhaps, recognize.[80]

Many things can go wrong in a nuclear attack. Both sides test their missiles on a trajectory spanning laterally across the globe. Nobody has tested one going over the North Pole, which is the path the missiles would travel in a real attack. The gravitational pull over the Borealis region is different from that over the Pacific Ocean. Weapons technicians say they allow for this difference and compute it into their calculations of accuracy; but there are a great many uncertainties about gravity, geoditic influences and so forth, and nobody would discover the real differences and effects until they launched a first strike.

Neither side really knows the *precise* accuracy of its weapons, not even the precise explosive yield, and surely not the precise hardness of the other side's missile silos. Yet calculations of kill-probability—that is, calculations assessing the success or failure of a first strike against silos—hinge on precise estimates of these factors. Anything less than precision can lead to calamity.

Other uncertainties abound, some of them esoteric but no less critical to success in a first-strike escapade. One of the most critical is "fratricide." It is generally assumed by analysts that two warheads are needed to maximize the likelihood of knocking out a missile silo (just as two gunshots increase the chances of hitting the bull's-eye on a target range). Yet effects of nuclear explosions include scattered neutrons, considerable debris, very high wind velocities, and a thick radioactive cloud of various particles swooped up from the ground. If another warhead came in shortly after the first, these effects would probably cause the second or third to explode prematurely, to be blown off target, to burn away much of its nuclear material and create a much smaller explosive yield, or to be destroyed itself. And the thick radioactive cloud could impede a second warhead from accomplishing its task for up to one hour after the first

43

explosion.[81]

Other little things could go wrong: the fuse might not work properly—if it were just a fraction of a second off it could wreck the entire attack plan. The same is true for minor errors in the re-entry angle and slightly poor timing in the workings of hundreds of electronic parts and engine generators.[82]

Then there is the *ultimate* uncertainty: Soviet leaders would never know whether the United States would launch its ICBMs on warning as soon as its radar observed Soviet missiles coming over the horizon, in which case Soviet warheads would strike only empty holes, and the Soviet leadership would face the grim prospect of being devastated by all-out U.S. retaliation.[83]

In short, computer models of missile effects indicate that the United States Minuteman force will become alarmingly vulnerable by the early to mid-1980s. However, these models have never been tested in real life; and a political or military leader would have to be overlooking an enormous package of uncertainties to order an attack based on theoretical calculations. To do so would require great irrationality; yet the whole theory of deterrence hinges on rational leaders, the proposition that a leader would not lead his society and state to virtually certain suicide. This may be a false premise; but if it is, then the entire rationale of having nuclear weapons collapses, and the vulnerability of our ICBM force has little to do with the theory's demise.

Does ICBM Vulnerability Matter?

Even if a highly limited computer model's view of the world is seen as legitimate—for the flimsy reason that "it's all we've got"—then one must still ask whether the problem of Minuteman vulnerability is something worth worrying much about.

It must be emphasized that land-based ICBMs do not constitute the entire U.S. strategic nuclear arsenal. As Defense Secretary Harold Brown points out, Minuteman vulnerability "would not be synonymous with the vulnerability of the United States, or even of the strategic deterrent. It would not mean that we could not satisfy our strategic objectives."[84] The United States, after all,

44

Even if the Soviets could execute a splendid first strike against the American ICBM force, they would still be faced with roughly 5000 strategic nuclear warheads that could thoroughly blast away the foundations of 20th century Soviet society, or destroy political, economic and military targets with flexibility and selectivity.

carries only about 22 percent of its strategic nuclear warheads on ICBMs.[85] As cruise missiles and Trident submarines enter the force, this percentage will diminish still further. Even if the Soviets could execute a splendid first strike against the American ICBM force, they would still be faced with roughly 5000 strategic nuclear warheads that could thoroughly blast away the foundations of 20th century Soviet society, or destroy political, economic and military targets with flexibility and selectivity.

This final point is important because it's where the "Planner's Nightmare" falls apart completely. In that scenario, Minuteman vulnerability is deemed catastrophic because, without the ICBMs, we could retaliate against a Soviet first strike only by hitting their cities; and we would not do that because the Soviets, with their fairly large reserve forces, would then strike back at our own cities—thus, rather than jeopardize 100-million or so American citizens, we would do nothing. But, if we have the capability to strike back at targets other than cities, and to do so selectively, the nightmare scenario collapses and thus the reason for concern about ICBM vulnerability vanishes. *And we do have that capability*—in the 150 or so ICBM warheads that would survive an attack, along with the thousands of gravity bombs, cruise missiles and SLBM warheads. True, the SLBM warheads are not yet accurate enough to strike at Soviet missile silos; but they're perfectly adequate for destroying air bases, submarine pens, naval ports, army depots and other similar targets. As Harold Brown notes,

45

even after a total loss of Minuteman missiles, we would *not* face the dilemma of surrender by inaction or mutual suicide by an all-out attack on Soviet cities and industry, provoking an equal attack on ours. We would instead have surviving bomber and submarine forces still fully capable of selectively attacking military, economic and control targets, *thus negating any gain the Soviets might imagine they could attain by an attack on our ICBM force.*[86]

Now, running the scenario by again, but correcting the fallacious assumption regarding the flexibility of the remaining forces, we find: the Soviets launch a first strike attack against our ICBMs; but instead of surrendering, we respond by knocking out a substantial portion of a particular sector of their economy or military forces, and then *we* tell *them:* "Don't retaliate or else *we'll* respond by annihilating *your* cities."

There is, of course, something unreal about this tit-for-tat, limited-nuclear-war game. Once nuclear warheads start flying around, command and control over the weapons will probably break down; the "hot line" will probably fail; things will, in short, get very much out of hand. Even Harold Brown acknowledges that once nuclear weapons start exploding, the chance of keeping things limited is very low. "Nuclear war-termination" is something nobody really knows much about.[87]

If, however, it is the hawks' contention that we have no flexibility in response were the bulk of our ICBMs to be destroyed, if the prime fear is that the USSR can play limited-nuclear-options while we cannot and that, therefore, we are helpless because we cannot "control escalation" as much as the Soviets can, then this claim—this fundamental assumption that drives the great panic over ICBM vulnerability—can be discarded as simply untrue.

The nightmare scenario depends, finally, on the reluctance and ultimately the failure of the President of the United States to retaliate after a Soviet nuclear attack. Yet even if the Soviets aimed just to destroy U.S. ICBMs, bomber bases and submarine ports without intending to kill a single civilian, radioactive fallout and other effects of nuclear weapons would kill somewhere between 2 and

20 million—most likely about 14 million—Americans.[88] Such a massacre is unprecedented in all of American history, and only rarely equalled in world history. To think that an American President would not retaliate after such unthinkable slaughter would require a most peculiar form of lunacy.

Actually, Paul Nitze and many others who take the ICBM-vulnerability threat seriously would agree with most of this. Most of them do not really believe that the Soviets will attack the United States with hundreds of nuclear warheads; they realize that the risks are simply too high. What really worries them is that possessing the capability to destroy our ICBM force might give the Soviets some sort of *political* advantage. They say that in some future Cuban Missile-type crisis, the Soviet superiority in throw-weight and counterforce power would force *the United States* to back down this time around; that the *perception* of this advantage, held by America's allies and foes, would have enormous impact in the international political arena; that our friends will feel compelled to rely less on our power and to move closer to the Soviet camp; and that the overall "correlation of forces" will favor the USSR.[89]

There are many problems with this argument. The analogy to the Cuban Missile Crisis, while perhaps superficially alarming, is not very apt upon inspection. In October 1962, the USSR had about thirty nuclear warheads of intercontinental range; now, and through the 1980s at least, the United States—even under the most pessimistic of circumstances—would have thousands of warheads, far more sophisticated than the Soviet weapons of the early 1960s and capable of raining destruction all over the Soviet Union.

The whole issue of "perceptions" is filled with irony. Those who play up the importance of perceptions are the same people who broadcast worldwide that the United States is inferior and who use misleading indicators (throw-weight, megatonnage, and so forth) and out-landish scenarios (ICBM vulnerability) to support their case. Indeed it is the heralders of Soviet "superiority" who have been *creating* these very perceptions. Who will claim that ordinary citizens and political leaders taught

47

themselves that, say, throw-weight is the chief indicator of strategic power? It wasn't our NATO allies or the President of the United States who first took a bomb-damage calculator out of the drawer and explored some nuclear-exchange models. Very little in Soviet military literature reflects emphasis on ICBM vulnerability or nuclear attacks confined to ICBM silos, and the Europeans showed no signs of nervousness about the situation until some of our own defense analysts pointed out the problems to them. In a written response to a question posed in hearings by Sen. John Culver (D-Ia.) concerning allied perceptions of U.S. military strength, the Defense Department noted that our allies

> ... sometimes, as individual nations, indicate that they would like to see some different allocations of our resources, but *they do not cite any perceived examples of current or potential weaknesses.*[90]

If the problem is one of perceptions, then it is a problem of our own making.

What Should We Do

"If it's vulnerable on paper, fix it"—that's the maxim employed by many, and so they urge that something be done about ICBM vulnerability, for if one leg of the U.S. strategic Triad appears to be vulnerable, then the Soviets might be tempted to try to destroy it in a desperate preemptive strike. This is the source of pressure for the MX missile system—or, precisely, the multiple-shelter basing mode for that missile.

Dozens of various mobile basing ideas have been considered over the past dozen years to ensure the "survivability" of our ICBMs. Last August, the President finally chose the relatively new "race-track" concept: a missile and its transporter-erector-launcher (TEL) would move around on a specially constructed, ovular-shaped road. Branching off from the road are 23 evenly spaced "spokes" with horizontal blast-resistant shelters into which the missile and its TEL can fit. The idea is if the Soviets wanted to knock out the 200 MX missiles, they would have to fire warheads at all 4,600 shelters, not knowing which really contains the missile.

This scheme will surely give land-based missiles a few more years of protection, but there are problems in the long run. First, there is "fractionation." This involves taking the payload of a missile and splitting it up, so to speak, into additional, though smaller, warheads. The Soviet SS-18 ICBM, currently with 10 warheads of 600 kilotons each, could be fitted with 25 of 200 kilotons or 30 to 40 of 50 kilotons.[91] The Air Force concedes that the Soviets could fractionate an additional warhead at roughly the same cost it would take for the United States to construct an additional shelter.[92] Thus, the Soviets could race the United States, warheads against shelters, at no cost penalty.

True, the SALT II treaty prohibits fractionation of ICBM warheads beyond 10 per missile;[93] but the treaty expires in 1985 (if, indeed, it is ever adopted), and the MX will not start deployment until 1986 or be fully deployed until 1989 or 1990.[94] Indeed, if the United States fully commits itself to a weapon system estimated to cost at least $33 billion, and if the effectiveness of this system requires the Soviets to stick to a fractionation limit in some arms-control treaty, then this will give the Soviets great leverage at SALT III, for they would know that Washington would do just about anything to hang onto the 10-warhead limit.

Furthermore, if the U.S. aim is to reduce the number of Soviet MIRVed ICBMs—that is, to create incentives for reductions in the most threatening of all Soviet weapons—then a multiple-shelter system is precisely the way to encourage the opposite. If the Soviets intend to go after American ICBMs, then multiplying the number of shelters to be hit only provides incentives for the Soviets to build up their MIRV force to even larger numbers. One lesson of recent history is that the Soviets will tend to do whatever it takes to perpetuate some military capability they deem important. (An example of this dedication lies in their continental air defense program. The Soviets have spent 12 to 15 percent of their defense budget each year for the past decade on air defense;[95] yet according to General Richard Ellis, Commander-in-Chief of the Strategic Air Command, American B-52 bombers, modified with

49

much cheaper avionics improvement, will still have a 75 percent chance of penetrating Soviet airspace by 1985.[96] The air-launched cruise missiles will nullify the Soviet effort altogether. The Soviets would have to spend an additional $30 to $50 billion over the next several years to threaten U.S. cruise missiles, and then some cheap matchbox-sized electronic modifications would render that expenditure totally useless.[97])

Or, if the Soviets did not further fractionate their ICBM warheads, they could develop very accurate SLBM warheads which could target the shelters. Indeed, it is probably only a matter of time before this happens.

Weaknesses in the race-track system abound. What if the Soviets somehow found out which shelter holds the MX? Couldn't they, using fairly accurate SLBMs launched from very close off American shores, either destroy the shelter before the missile could get out, or by using a cluster of warheads, blast the area of road surrounding the shelter, thus pinning the missile in, and then destroying it with ICBM warheads? Or, before the attack, couldn't Russian agents sabotage the whole system by blasting the roads with dynamite? (Only the points around the shelters will be marked off by security; the roads and surrounding areas are to be open to the public for picnicking or whatever.)

Finally, what if the Soviets developed their own multiple-shelter system or, worse still, an on-the-road mobile system? Conservative defense analysts in this country would constantly be on the lookout for "break-out"—that is, for the Soviets' filling in the holes with more missiles some night. This is a problem that goes beyond mere questions of arms-control verification; it strikes at the heart of rational defense planning. If the United States had no way of knowing how many ICBMs the Soviets have, then it could not know how many warheads the multiple-shelter system would have to "soak up"; thus, the United States could not know how many empty shelters to build for each missile, and therefore could not plan the system rationally. "Breakout gaps" would become inevitable in conservative defense thinking.

In short, multiple shelters will smooth over the ICBM vulnerability problem—to the extent that it is a problem—

*An alternative solution to the ICBM-
vulnerability problem is merely to
phase out land-based missiles
altogether . . .*

for a few years; but it will not solve the problem, at least so
long as the Soviets keep American ICBMs on their own
nuclear target list. Many Air Force and Pentagon officials
fool themselves into thinking that the Soviets will not
make the effort to keep up with us on this; that after seeing
the multiple-shelter system, the Soviets will give up and
undertake negotiations to get rid of ICBMs altogether.
But to believe such claims is only to indulge in what
Herbert York once called "the fallacy of the final step."[98]
Once again, U.S. defense planners fail to foresee the
dynamics that their own weapons-deployment decisions
generate.

Another solution, one posed by independent defense
analysts Richard Garwin and Sidney Drell of IBM and
Stanford respectively, is to put the missiles on small
submersibles to travel underwater up and down the
Atlantic and Pacific coastlines, not far from the shores.[99]
This would be a truly mobile solution, not one merely
involving multiple but fixed shelters. It would be spread
out over hundreds of thousands of miles of "aim points;"
and unlike Polaris, Poseidon and Trident nuclear-missile
submarines, stationed all over the ocean, the submersibles' proximity to the coastline would make command-
control-communications more reliable. On all scores, this
seems the sensible solution to the problem, if one
considers it a problem worthy of solution. Yet it also seems
bureaucratically the least likely. The Navy doesn't want
it; they are already spending an enormous amount of their
budget on strategic systems, particularly the Trident
submarine at $1.5 billion each. The Air Force doesn't want
it, having no desire to get into the business of designing
submarines. It's an idea that will probably live only in the
minds of a few creative analysts. There's no room for it
elsewhere.

An alternative solution to the ICBM-vulnerability   51

problem is merely to phase out land-based missiles altogether, and to improve the other two legs of the Triad—by putting more cruise missiles on bombers, by upgrading command-control-communications with submarines, and by increasing the accuracy of submarine-launched missiles. If ICBMs are becoming truly vulnerable, then now may be the time to shift the concentration of U.S. forces to other platforms. Phasing out land-based missiles would also make the Continental United States less vulnerable to nuclear attack, and would make much of the large Soviet ICBM force—designed, in part, to destroy the Minuteman force—rather superfluous.

The race-track scheme or similar multiple-shelter designs on land are the wrong way to go for a number of reasons. They are very expensive, they encourage the Soviets to expand the most dangerous component of their strategic force, and they will eventually be matched by the Soviets if American analysts are correct in assuming that the USSR is going after our ICBMs. Eventually, the United States will almost certainly be forced to place the bulk of its weapons in the air and out to sea, anyway; surely it would be most sensible to skip one whole new stage of the arms race, and to head that way now.

Summary of Soviet Capabilities

There is no doubt that the Soviets are increasing their strategic power. They spend more than the United States does, they have more missiles than we do, their missiles are heavier than ours, they seem to spend and write more on civil defense, and their ICBM warheads are growing in number and accuracy to the point that our own ICBMs will, at least theoretically, become vulnerable by the early to mid-1980s. Nevertheless, the question must be asked: How significant are these trends? Will the United States still, for the foreseeable future, be able to carry out its strategic missions and to deter Soviet attack?

Measuring Soviet military expenditures in dollars carries a strong upward bias, as the CIA readily admits; measuring them in Russian rubles makes spending levels appear much more equal. Further, Soviet strategic programs are far more inefficient than U.S. programs;

indeed, our expenditures in nuclear weapons over the past decade have been about five times as cost-effective as Soviet spending.

Those pointing to Soviet numerical superiority in missiles and bombers point only at the irrelevant. The United States has 50 percent more warheads and bombs (the things that actually kill people and demolish targets); and in any event, both sides have more than enough to deter the other from nuclear adventurism.

True, Soviet missiles are heavier than American ones, but Soviet missile design is far less efficient; compared with the USSR, it takes far fewer pounds of payload for the United States to get equal explosive yield. Soviet missiles also have more megatons than American missiles; but megatonnage (or equivalent megatonnage) is only a good measure for destruction of area, whereas both sides' targeting strategies aim to destroy individual military or industrial facilities, rather than to bust up cities or do indiscriminate damage to territory. As missiles become increasingly accurate, explosive yield has increasingly diminishing impact on determining whether the warhead will destroy its intended target.

Some believe that a Soviet civil defense program will radically reduce the damage done to the USSR's economy, but there is no evidence supporting this claim and much evidence to refute it. The supreme difficulties of planning a mass evacuation and sheltering program—as well as the insurmountable contradiction between the industrial dispersion and protection needed for an effective civil defense program on the one hand, and the heavily bottle-necked, concentrated and centralized Soviet economy on the other hand—make it a remarkably unreliable hedge on which an aggressive Soviet leader could depend for protection against an American retaliatory nuclear strike.

Finally, while calculations suggest that American ICBMs will be vulnerable to a Soviet first strike by the early to mid-1980s, the model on which these calculations are based is highly abstract, divorced from the numerous uncertainties facing any military planner in real life. Even if the missiles were truly vulnerable, this fact is not very significant: land-based missiles constitute only 22 percent of the U.S. strategic arsenal; the thousands of other SLBM warheads, gravity bombs and cruise missiles could devastate Soviet society or, if the President chose, could respond to Soviet limited attacks with deliberate flexibility and selectivity. And if one is still worried about ICBM vulnerability after considering all this, the best solution may be to phase out the land-based missile force altogether and to make improvements in the other two "legs" of the Strategic Triad. In any event, moving toward a multiple-shelter system on land—such as the "race-track" basing scheme proposed for the MX missile—is the wrong way to go for a variety of reasons.

In short, there are few grounds for complacency about the Soviets; they are improving their forces more, and more quickly, than intelligence analysts had predicted just a few years ago. However, neither are there grounds for panic. The American deterrent force remains secure and strong; notions of impending Soviet "strategic superiority" have no operational meaning. We are still able to carry out our strategic missions, we can still deter the Soviets from attacking, and we can respond in limited fashion to limited strikes. As long as this is so, there is a "strategic balance."

III:
THE SOVIET VIEW:
AN AMERICAN
THREAT?

The Threat game is one that thrives on both sides, making it, however elusive, a political fact of life. From the Soviet viewpoint, a glance at official U.S. literature and at various weapons systems under development could reveal signs of U.S. "superiority seeking" as well. When asked if he could make the United States seem a threatening aggressor were he working for the Kremlin High Command, one Pentagon planner responded, "Oh sure, I could paint a pretty scary picture."

The new Mark-12A warhead, three of which will be placed on each of 300 Minuteman III ICBMs over the next two years, will have an 83 percent chance of destroying a Soviet missile silo in a single shot by the mid-1980s—the same "kill-probability" assigned to the most advanced Soviet ICBM warheads of that time.[1] The MX, to be deployed in 1986, with the Mark-12A and an Advanced Inertial Reference Sphere (AIRS) inertial guidance system—allowing accuracies of 300 feet—will have a 97 percent single-shot kill-probability against Soviet silos.[2] The air-launched cruise missile will destroy anything it is fired at with virtual certainty, no matter how blast-resistant the target. And the Trident II missile, coming along in the late 1980s, with 14 warheads of roughly 150 kilotons and very good accuracy, will be highly capable against Soviet silos as well.[3]

U.S. Defense Department officials deny that these weapons give the United States anything like "strategic superiority," or that the Soviets should look at highly accurate U.S. warheads as "destabilizing," because, after all, the Soviet Union would still have its submarine missiles and bombers that could wipe out the American industrial base.[4]

These officials may be right, but if that argument applies to America's counterforce capability, why should it not also apply to Soviet counterforce weapons? Indeed, *the Soviets have more reason to fear ICBM vulnerability,* since more than 70 percent of its warheads are on ICBMs, compared with 22 percent of American strategic nuclear warheads.[5] Given the pace of Soviet MIRVed ICBM programs, this percentage will certainly increase for the USSR—whereas, given cruise missiles and Trident submarines, it will certainly decrease for the U.S. Improvements in missile accuracy, in other words, endanger a much larger proportion of Soviet forces compared with the danger to American forces.

Recent reports released by the U.S. Defense Advanced Research Projects Agency (DARPA) would not assure the Russians much, either. DARPA, whose sole mission is to devise technological breakthroughs and to seek military applications for their scientific wonders, is coming up with some marvelous devices, particularly in the area of anti-submarine warfare (ASW). The authors of its annual report excitedly invite the reader to "ponder the consequences of an ability to not only detect but to localize and track quiet submarines at long range." They state: "As long as a large portion of the SSBN [nuclear ballistic-missile submarine] force can avoid continuous surveillance, a successful preemptive strike is not possible." This is certainly correct. They then proceed to describe their plans to make continuous surveillance—and presumably a "successful preemptive strike"—possible.[6]

The Soviets obviously spend much time and money on ASW projects as well. But U.S. intelligence analysts report that the Soviets have not been successful on a single ASW project—at least on any wide-ocean application of ASW technology. Even if the Soviets did latch on to the right technology, geography would be a monumental restriction to their successful operations.[7] This geographic disadvantage is exacerbated by American deployment of the Trident I missile, which will replace older

DARPA's work is approved by the top, and a Soviet military planner reading the reports coming from the agency would not be unreasonably "paranoid" for concluding that at least some high-ranking Defense Department officials are aiming for a first-strike capability against the Soviet Union.

missiles in 12 of the 31 Poseidon submarines over the next two years, and be fitted into the 24 tubes on each Trident submarine. The Trident I has a range of 4000 nautical miles, compared with the 2600 nautical-mile range of the Poseidon. This extra range expands the area of ocean from which U.S. submarines can operate and still hit their targets in the Soviet Union by 10 to 20 times.[8]

It should be pointed out that the scientists at DARPA do not always reflect consensus thinking at the top; but all of DARPA's work is approved by the top, and a Soviet military planner reading the reports coming from the agency would not be unreasonably "paranoid" for concluding that at least some high-ranking Defense Department officials are aiming for a first-strike capability against the Soviet Union.

As for civil defense, most America-watchers in the USSR must realize that a serious U.S. program does not really exist, just as most Russia-watchers in the U.S. realize that the Soviet program—though taken more seriously by more people—is a fatally flawed program for anything but marginal protection against a very limited (e.g., accidental or China-launched) attack. However, grounds exist for thinking otherwise. According to the U.S. Defense Civil Preparedness Agency, there are identified shelter spaces for 230 million Americans and existing plans to protect 85 percent of the population in case of nuclear attack. Civil defense manuals are in print for virtually every industrial sector in the economy.[9] Many private analysts with government contracts, such as Herman Kahn of the Hudson Institute (whom one Soviet publication describes as "an ideologue of U.S.

imperialism," whose "morbid misanthropic books . . . have become manuals for Pentagon's military planning"), have spelled out the "feasibility and desirability of widespread evacuation and sheltering."[10] All of this may be nonsense—but grounds for Soviet anxiety nevertheless, just as much nonsense about Soviet civil defense has furnished grounds for some American anxiety.

Finally, the U.S. has several thousand theater nuclear weapons in Europe and on aircraft carriers that have the range necessary to strike Soviet territory.[11] The USSR has 3,500 theater nuclear weapons in Europe as well, but none of them can hit the United States. Furthermore, the United States now plans to upgrade its theater nuclear forces by deploying the Pershing II Extended Range missile and the Ground Launched Cruise Missile (GLCM)—with 1000- and 1500-kilometer ranges respectively, or enough to strike the Soviet Union from Western Europe. Pershing II and the GLCM are intended as responses to modern Soviet theater weapons, particularly the SS-20 missile, launched from inside the USSR and intended to strike Western Europe; still, the SS-20 cannot hit the United States, and this "asymmetry" must surely be apparent to the Soviets.

None of this is to say that the United States will soon emerge with "strategic superiority," or that American attempts to launch a first strike would not fail as dismally as would Soviet attempts. The point is merely that the spiralling arms race is fueled by—and, in turn, promotes—*mutual* fear and uncertainty between the United States and the Soviet Union. Each new move by one side creates new fears and uncertainties on the other side. Moreover, it is worth noting that, while in some instances the Soviets have surpassed the United States in the number of some of these new systems, the United States has, often shortsightedly, been the side that has more often moved first in the deployment of new weapons and new military technologies.

IV:
SALT AND
THE FUTURE
OF ARMS CONTROL

Liberals and conservatives alike have become rather disillusioned with the Strategic Arms Limitation Talks—liberals because so few strategic arms actually get limited, conservatives because the results have done little to ward off the Soviet threat as they perceive it.

SALT I, signed in May 1972, may actually have propelled more arms into existence than it restricted or prohibited (with the highly noteworthy exception of the ABM Treaty). In hearings held shortly after the agreement was signed, Defense Secretary Melvin Laird gave the Senate an instructive document entitled "SALT Related Adjustments to Strategic Programs," which listed revised budget requests deemed necessary as a result of SALT I restrictions. These adjustments were not for restraint, but for expansion and acceleration of weaponry: "Accelerate and complete development of site defense"; "Develop submarine-launched cruise missiles"; "Develop improved [accuracy] re-entry vehicles for ICBMs and SLBMs"; and acclerate spending on the Trident submarine, which the Senate Armed Services, up to that point, had refused to fund.[1] Arms-control scholars George Rathjens, Jack Ruina and Abram Chayes were moved to comment:

> The wry joke is heard that SALT may be a great boon for weapons procurement: a mechanism for generating and sustaining support for new weapons programs at a time when the domestic climate is such that they would

SALT I, signed in May 1972, may actually have propelled more arms into existence than it restricted or prohibited (with the highly noteworthy exception of the ABM Treaty).... The same cannot be said for SALT II.

otherwise be in jeopardy.[2]

The same cannot be said for SALT II. The "domestic climate" does not jeopardize many new weapons systems, as it did when Rathjens, Ruina and Chayes were writing in 1974. Quite the contrary: Public opinion today is very receptive to rapid weapons deployment. A few years ago, the Senate debated whether to raise or reduce defense spending; in 1978, the debate was whether to increase it by one percent or three percent; last year, it was whether to go with three percent real growth or five percent; now, in the wake of the Soviet Union's Christmastime invasion of Afghanistan, some Senators are talking about the need for 10 percent growth in the defense budget, and congressional opposition to major strategic weapons systems has virtually collapsed. "ICBM vulnerability" has entered the common vocabulary; "Soviet strategic superiority" is a concept and an assessment rarely contested. SALT II lies on the back burner—and even those flames have been extinguished, perhaps for good.

While the SALT debate was the hot issue in Washington, some liberal Democratic Senators were correct to complain that the treaty allowed the United States to proceed with the MX missile, the Trident systems, all sorts of cruise missiles and much else. However, they were wrong to suggest that SALT II *caused* development or deployment of those systems.[3] They were planned in the early 1970s; they would almost certainly have been proposed by the Administration and accepted by the Congress, with or without SALT II (and with or without the Afghanistan invasion).[4] SALT II, if it is ever ratified, offers a number of virtues. It *reduces* weaponry for the first time; it limits not only missiles, but also

60

warheads; and it "bounds" the threat—it makes the Soviet threat more predictable for U.S. defense planners and the American threat more predictable for Soviet planners. Predictability makes for more rational defense planning, "worst-case" estimates that are less wild, and thus defense budgets that are less extravagant than they otherwise would be. It has been estimated that without SALT II, the Soviets would probably deploy 3000 additional warheads, and spending for U.S. strategic programs would be $20 to $30 billion higher over the next decade than would be the case with SALT II. A recent CIA National Intelligence Estimate, obviously leaked to the press by the White House, notes that by 1989 the Soviets could deploy up to 8000 more ICBM warheads alone without SALT II than with the treaty.[5]

However, the whole "SALT process" has failed, and is bound to continue failing, in two ways: First, it has distorted the defense debate; second, it has not solved the fundamental problems that concern defense analysts of virtually all persuasion.

First, SALT has distorted the debate by focussing excessively on issues that would otherwise be rightly dismissed or ignored as trivial. For example, SALT limits strategic launchers because the number of launchers is the easiest thing for a treaty to control and for intelligence analysts to monitor and verify. This prompts many Senators and citizens to believe that launchers are an important indicator of the strategic balance, whereas in the age of MIRVs, they mean little. When SALT II finally gets around to controlling "new types" of weapons systems, the negotiators choose throw-weight as the measure to control because, again, it is the most easily verifiable. This prompts many to believe that throw-weight is a critical indicator—an area in which the Soviets are far ahead, but, as we have seen, whose significance is nil.

Broadly speaking, SALT promotes assessments of the strategic balance based on comparisons of static indicators. Yet "bean-counting" has little to do with realistic views of the balance or of deterrence. Defense policy theoretically hinges on several planning factors: What is U.S. defense policy? What purposes should

One way to slow down the arms race would be to limit the number of test-flights each side can conduct—to, perhaps, six per year.

nuclear weapons serve? How many are needed for that purpose? What should be deployed, and what should be restricted, to enhance national security? What level of damage must the Soviets inflict on U.S. nuclear forces in order to prevent them from carrying out their strategic missions? Can the Soviets, now or in the foreseeable future, wreak such damage; and if so, what should we do about it? These are questions rarely posed by policy-makers these days; and, to a large extent, this failure is exacerbated by the "SALT process," with its inordinate concentration on static indicators that—however important they may be for arms control negotiations and verification—are of little importance to considerations of the real-life nuclear balance. This distortion of defense issues and strategy may be SALT's most deadly legacy.

Meanwhile, the important indicators of missile capability—yield and accuracy—are difficult to control because they are difficult to monitor, and thus verify, precisely. Neither side, with good reason, seems willing to negotiate a treaty that cannot be adequately verified by independent technical means.

It is difficult, as well, to control research and development of new strategic programs—where everything begins—because they, too, are difficult to verify. Besides, many improvements in strategic weapons spring from developments in conventional weapons or civilian projects. For example, improvements in missile guidance systems are the offspring, by and large, of developments in navigational systems for commercial aircraft—and thus are very difficult to control through strategic arms control agreements alone.[6]

However, if the key worry involves the development of new weapons systems that may destabilize the military balance by endangering all three legs of each side's strategic Triad or its warning systems, then there may be *indirect* ways of controlling the spiralling escalation of arms.

For example, each side must test a new missile 15 or 20 times before it is operationally reliable. One way to slow down the arms race would be to limit the number of test-flights each side can conduct—to, perhaps, six per year.[7] Currently, both sides periodically test currently deployed systems just to ensure they are still in working order. A limit of six test-flights per year for each side would be enough to assure the continued reliability of weapons already fielded, but not enough to do much in the testing of new systems. The limit would require prolonging the development stage of a new missile by several years—plenty of time to let the other side react if the new system appeared to endanger security.

Another possibility, suggested by Representatives Bob Carr and Thomas Downey, is to prohibit testing of SLBMs in a depressed-trajectory—i.e., in a flight-path that has a very low arch.[8] If a nuclear-missile submarine moved in close to the enemy's shores and launched a missile in depressed trajectory, it could hit a bomber base within as little as five minutes, allowing no time for bombers to escape, and thus (if the missiles were also accurate) taking out most of the ICBMs and all the bombers simultaneously. Because depressed trajectories distort the accuracy of a missile somewhat, it would take two or three years of testing for a nation's weapons designers to measure and make all the adjustments necessary for making the missile perform as intended.[9] A ban on such testing would do much to promote strategic stability.

A related measure might be a ban on the deployment by either side of its nuclear-missile submarines (SSBNs) within a few hundred miles of the other's shorelines. This would also prevent the quick SLBM strike that could take out the ICBMs and bombers at once (even if the missiles were launched in a normal rather than depressed trajectory).

Some thought might also be given to creating "SSBN sanctuaries"—i.e., areas of the ocean, close to both sides' coastlines, in which ASW ships, sonobuoys or other such equipment of the other side could not be placed in any form.

Some analysts worry about the vulnerability of our early-warning satellites, which would be needed to relay messages of a Soviet attack. Much fuss was aroused a couple years ago when the Soviets began testing anti-satellite (ASAT) devices. They would send up a satellite, direct it to a point near another satellite, then pull it away and explode it to bits. The threat was clear: had they wanted to do so, they could have destroyed the other satellite as well, and the other satellite could have been American. To counter this new Soviet capability the United States, which had stopped work on an anti-satellite system in the mid-1960s, embarked upon a renewed ASAT effort. In fact, however, the Soviet ASAT program is not very successful. It has worked in only about half the tests, and then only at altitudes of a few hundred feet—whereas U.S. early-warning satellites are stationed at more than 10,000 feet in space.[10]*

It would, admittedly, be very difficult to conduct ASAT limitation talks because the Soviets and the Americans are going about their efforts in totally different ways: The Soviets use "killer satellites"; the United States, on the other hand, plans to use Miniature Homing Vehicles, which can be carried close to outer space by supersonic F-15 jet fighters and then launched, whereupon they home in on enemy satellites.[11] The United States is not about to place ceilings on the number of F-15s (vital for conventional air-to-air warfare), or to stop its Space Shuttle program, another *potential* plat-

---

*ASAT programs chiefly threaten reconaissance and communications satellites that would aid NATO or Warsaw Pact forces in a conventional war in Europe or at sea. Dr. Seymour Zeiberg, Deputy Under Secretary of Defense for Strategic and Space Systems, defends development of an American ASAT system because "the Soviets have satellites in their force which can track, locate, and assist in the targeting of elements of our military forces . . . So we ought to have in our back pocket the capabilities to negate those satellites in times of war as appropriate." (Senate Armed Services Committee, Authorization Hearings, FY 1980, Pt. 6, p. 3027.) Unfortunately, both the U.S. and the USSR are relying increasingly on satellites for target acquisition and communications, and so long as this remains true, ASAT seems a dangerously logical development.

64

form for ASAT activity that also has other (non-military) functions. One possible way of controlling the damage these systems can do to strategic warning, however, is to place limits on how high each side can conduct ASAT tests, and to make this ceiling far below the altitude of early-warning satellites.

These approaches may contribute to strategic stability; but what about disarmament, real reductions in weapons, particularly in the number of MIRVed ICBMs, the source of most of this instability?

Some arms control advocates have offered radical and direct solutions to this problem. One technique, known as Percent Annual Reductions (PAR), would have both sides reduce their number of MIRVed ICBMs by five or ten percent annually over a period of a few years until the systems are down to zero in number.[12] A nice approach if you could get it, but that doesn't seem likely. This approach neglects the fact that both sides have as part of their "target packages" the destruction of the other's ICBM silos; and the most efficient way of executing that mission is by using MIRVed ICBMs. With multiple independently targetable warheads, one missile can theoretically destroy several of the other side's missile silos; and with ICBMs, the task can be accomplished more rapidly and reliably. Reductions in MIRV weapons are feasible up to a point because a dynamic element is involved: for each ICBM that one side dismantles, that's one less ICBM that the other needs to target; however, for each, say, six-warhead SS-19 that the Soviets dismantle, that's six fewer targets that the Soviets can destroy. Thus, one-for-one trade-offs in MIRVed ICBM reductions seem unlikely beyond a certain point—*unless one or both sides change their targeting strategies.* This is crucial; without a full understanding of this dimension, arms-control efforts will inevitably deliver far less than they promise.

V:
STRATEGY
IN PERSPECTIVE

And so we conclude where we began, and where all discussions of nuclear weapons must begin and conclude—with *strategy*.

Recall for a moment that McNamara and his systems analysts officially set the criterion of "mutual assured destruction" as the capability to destroy about 25 to 30 percent of the Soviet population and half or so of its industrial base, and calculated (rather arbitrarily) that this required 400 equivalent megatons in the surviving U.S. arsenal after the most effective conceivable Soviet first strike against America's strategic forces. In fact, McNamara really had counterforce strategies in mind, but the Soviet force was at that time so small that it could be wiped out with weapons no larger in number, and no better in design, than those needed for a strategy for destroying cities. As the Soviet arsenal grew, however, so necessarily did the U.S. force; and as the Soviets hardened their ICBMs in silos, so the U.S. made its weapons more accurate. In short, much of the development of the U.S. weapons over the past decade or so has been driven by the need to fulfill the requirements of a counterforce—and particularly a *counter-silo* strategy. Naturally, the Soviet Threat was cited as the reason for U.S. expansion and improvement; but while Soviet developments may have been responsible, they posed a threat mainly to America's ability to threaten strategic forces.

The official rationale for a U.S. counter-silo strategy goes like this: The United States needs to have a "prompt hard-target kill capability" because the Soviet Union has one, and we cannot allow this "asymmetry"—with its dreadful political, if not military consequences—to continue.

Three comments are necessary here. First, the Soviets have not developed this capability unilaterally. As noted elsewhere, the United States has always aimed its missiles at Soviet missiles; and presently, the U.S. and USSR are roughly equal in their ability to destroy the other side's strategic forces.[1]   Second, even if the claim were true, it does not make sense that just because the Soviets can knock out our ICBMs, we must be able to knock out theirs. Such knee-jerk mirror-imaging would only create a hair-trigger situation in which, during a particularly serious crisis, both sides—fearing the other might strike first—would be tempted to launch a pre-emptive strike. This is the *paramount danger* of a counterforce/counter-silo posture.

Finally, if the Soviets were so foolhardy as to fire some 2000 nuclear weapons at U.S. territory, it is very likely that they would launch most, if not all, of their remaining missiles on warning as their radar pick up several hundred of our ICBM warheads coming over the horizon—warheads that, because of their accuracy, the Soviets could safely assume were aimed against their own missile silos.

There is a good deal of evidence that the Soviets think seriously about launch-on-warning and launch-under-attack, and that they would almost certainly adopt such a posture if their ICBMs were on very high alert (as they assuredly would be after they had initiated a nuclear war). One former CIA analyst believes that the Soviets adopted a launch-on-warning posture in the late 1960s (which may explain the lack of concern in their own military writings over ICBM vulnerability).[2] Some Soviet literature confirms this theory.[3]

It makes no sense, then, to fire our surviving warheads against the residual Soviet ICBM force, only to waste them on empty holes. Moreover, the Soviets' remaining force would probably consist of missiles somewhat less accurate than those fired at Minuteman silos, and thus very likely targeted against America's manufacturing and administrative centers, most of which lie in the heart of our cities. In other words, in an effort to "limit damage" by knocking out the remaining Soviet ICBMs, the U.S. might instead *maximize* damage to U.S. territory.

If military planners still think it's worth the gamble to go ahead and try to blow up those remaining Soviet ICBMs anyway, they have not explained why ICBMs are necessary to do the job. Gravity bombs and, even more, air-launched cruise missiles could pull off the mission efficiently enough—cruise missiles with a higher kill-probability than the ICBMs. The usual counterargument to this is that cruise missiles would take eight hours or so to reach their targets, whereas ICBMs could do it in 25 or 30 minutes. *Prompt* hard-target kill is necessary, they say, because missile silos are *time-urgent* targets—that is, they could move (in this case, be launched) in a short period of time. This is true, but the Soviets could just as easily decide to launch the ICBMs with 25 minutes as with eight hours of warning. No theory or lesson of history or statement of doctrine suggests that the Soviets would be less likely to launch on warning with shorter warning time; 25 minutes is enough so that it could, physically, be done.

A case could be made that *some* hard targets ought to be among those hit in a retaliatory blow—for example nuclear storage sites, command posts, and so forth. These things, however, do not move, so they do not need to be destroyed *promptly*—or, if for some reason, they should be, the 100 or so surviving Minuteman missiles (which can be rapidly re-targeted from an air-based launch control center) would be enough to carry out the mission.[4]

Nuclear war planning is getting out of hand, this much is clear to all but those mind-numbingly engrossed in its otherworldly chessgame aspects. Few in the business have managed to hang on to first principles— namely, that the primary purpose of nuclear weapons is not to use them, and that their mere possession poses such an overwhelming threat that it deters all enemies from using them against us or threatening to do so.

Flexible options and a capacity for selective use of nuclear weapons are important to have (and the U.S. has

The world is becoming perilous enough . . . now is hardly the time for the two military giants to be sitting with nuclear strategies and weapons that promote hair-trigger solutions.

them in spades). While the promise of "assured destruction" of an aggressor's 200 largest cities probably carries the most palpably horrifying deterrent, nobody can claim to know what really constitutes deterrence with absolute confidence. If, for some reason, deterrence fails and nuclear war breaks out, the United States should (and does) have options other than to kill tens of millions of Russians and destroy their homes, factories and society in general. Even if chances are high that a limited nuclear war would escalate to one of all-out destruction, that does not mean the United States should respond to a limited nuclear attack in such a way as to *ensure* escalation, especially since the Soviet Union, after a first strike, would still have thousands of nuclear warheads remaining, most of them targeted against the United States.[5]

However, there is a difference between making provisions for flexible options and building forces for really fighting a nuclear war by threatening the bulk of the other side's nuclear forces.[6] However risky, both the United States and the Soviet Union are taking ever bigger steps toward the latter. And the fact that one of them does so first (whichever one that is) does not excuse the other from following in its footsteps; that makes the hair-trigger still tighter, and makes the chances of nuclear war still greater.

Before both sides grimly leap into still another round of the nuclear arms competition—with the United States developing the MX, the Trident II, and hosts of other hard-target killers, and with the Soviets developing a fifth generation of ICBMs and still more accurate guidance systems—it is time for both sides to reassess their targeting strategies, and to ask whether maintaining and improving counter-silo/counterforce strategies is worth the cost in dollars, rubles and strategic stability, espe-

69

cially in light of the potential futility of such strategies (given possibilities of launch-under-attack and other forms of preemption).

The world is becoming perilous enough. With growing Third World autonomy, potential oil shortages for both superpowers, upheaval in the Middle East, impending proxy wars in Africa, and a host of other problems, now is hardly the time for the two military giants to be sitting with nuclear strategies and weapons that promote hair-trigger final solutions.

The old questions must be asked again: What does it take to deter? What constitutes "unacceptable damage"? And if deterrence does fail, what is the best way to try to control escalation? Is it to destroy promptly the other side's missile silos? Probably not, if he's going to launch on warning if I try doing so, for that would only assure continued escalation. Wouldn't it be better, perhaps, to attack conventional military facilities or some industrial sites in the far outposts, with a message that much more will follow if he decides to launch any more nuclear weapons? If escalation can be controlled, it would only be because both sides recoil from Armageddon, come to their senses, and go to the negotiating tables. This approach—which requires no MX, no super-accurate warheads, little if any prompt-hard-target-kill capabilities, and no ICBMs for that matter—seems the safest, or least dangerous, solution to the problem. This sort of strategy for initial retaliation may not prevent escalation; it probably won't.* However, its consequences—a whole industry ripped asunder, or whole divisions of troops wiped out in a single blow, along with (unavoidably) the deaths of a few million civilians—would be sufficiently horrifying to any sane leader that its prospect would almost certainly deter nuclear attack. And it avoids both the bloodthirsty suicide of "mutual assured destruction" and the cold-blooded fantasy-land of disarming counter-silo tactics.

In any event, both sides must start to think more seriously about how best to prevent nuclear war and, in

---

*For one thing, Soviet military literature says nothing about nuclear firebreaks, tit-for-tat strategies, limited nuclear war or any of the other refinements mentioned in U.S. doctrine.

the event this cannot be managed, how best to stop it once it starts—*not* how to fight and win it. If nuclear war can be won, the victory would be so Pyrrhic as to be meaningless.

VI:
CONCLUSION AND A NOTE ON PERCEPTION

The specter of the Soviet Threat is, of course, nothing new. Since the beginnings of the Cold War, the American public has been barraged with ominous scenarios involving "bomber gaps," "missile gaps," and now a "throw-weight gap," a "civil defense gap" and a "counterforce gap." In the past, these fearsome phenomena—all of them gravely pronounced by government-sponsored, top-secret, blue-ribbon panels composed of eminent public figures—have proved highly exaggerated, sometimes downright false. The same can be said of many of the scare stories presently pervading much of the public consciousness on defense issues.

This is not to say there is nothing to worry about. The Soviets have been building up their military forces, and the Soviet build-up over the past decade has been greater than that of the U.S. Still, the United States has hardly been standing still: it has added 5,250 warheads to its strategic arsenal in the past decade, compared with the Soviets' 4,560 additional; it moved ahead on MIRVs five years before the Soviets got started, and quickly spread them out over ICBMs and SLBMs, whereas the Soviets started putting them on submarine-launched missiles in 1978; it hardened its missile silos by a factor of five or six, and tripled the hard-target kill capability of its most sophisticated ICBM system (the Soviets did about the same); and it continues to move ahead with air-launched cruise missiles (thus defeating the Soviets' extraordinarily expensive air defense system), long-range Trident I missiles (thus putting off for several more years the effectiveness of any possible, but currently non-existent, Soviet ASW breakthrough), and other systems. In sum, the Soviet effort of the past ten years has hardly antiquated the U.S. force or endangered deterrence or made Soviet superiority a definite thing to fear.[1]

As real as the Soviet Threat, perhaps even more so, is the specter of our own illusions. This is true in the area of conventional as well as nuclear forces. Edward Luttwak, hardly a dove, has wryly commented: "The Soviet Union has gained more than a mere psychological satisfaction from the widespread *impression* that her ground forces were vastly superior to those of the West." Luttwak points out, for example, that even though the mere number of armored divisions means little in terms of actual military strength,

> It is obvious that ... images of a superior Soviet army have derived from, and in degree have reflected, the superior number of Soviet divisions more than any other single index of ground-force capability . . . Virtually every press article touching on this issue includes a comparison of Warsaw Pact and NATO military strength cast in terms of divisional counts; few articles proceed to mention other indices ... Hardly any compare aggregate troop *quality* and force *quality*.[2]

Speaking of navies, Admiral Stansfield Turner, before becoming Director of Central Intelligence, noted similarly that

> the Soviets have been playing the game cleverly. Realizing that they are dealing with perceptions, they are gaining maximum advantage from the fact that any change is news. Small improvements in capability can be touted to the unsophisticated as big ones ... The invalidity of that claim is academic if it is universally believed.[3]

If perceptions play a strong role in shaping the military balance, one can only conclude that the constant bellowing about "Soviet superiority"—as articulated by 73

Paul Nitze, Richard Pipes, and many others—may do more damage to the image of American strength in the eyes of the world than all the throw-weight of all the heavy Soviet missiles combined. If perception is a key variable, then political leaders should attempt to change those perceptions.

This essay has attempted to shed some light on recent, highly publicized claims that the USSR is bound for "strategic superiority." Its thesis, in a nutshell, is that while the USSR *is* modernizing its military capabilities—and doing some things earlier and more quickly than the U.S. had anticipated a few years ago—this build-up does not and will not, for the foreseeable future, jeopardize the United States' ability to respond flexibly and selectively, or all-out, to Soviet nuclear strikes. Nor is there any credible evidence that the USSR could, short of U.S. diplomatic incompetence in the extreme, utilize its nuclear arsenal in campaigns of political intimidation or coercion—no more so now, or in the near future, than either side has been able to do since the early 1960s.

The Soviet Threat has been used, in part, to garner public and Congressional support for many new strategic weapons systems just moving into development—most notably the MX missile and its multiple-shelter basing scheme. If these new systems truly are meant to respond to Soviet moves, they are futile and dangerous gestures; futile because the USSR would soon be able to counter them, dangerous because rather than enhancing stability, they foster instability.

The issue of nuclear weapons—and, for that matter, conventional forces—should be seen in the context of overall missions and capabilities, not senseless bean-count comparisons; of outputs, not static inputs; of whether capabilities are sufficient to execute necessary missions. In the strategic nuclear weapons area, as long as the missions can reliably be fulfilled—and as long as this fact is made quite clear to all parties concerned—then the idea of "strategic superiority" is operationally meaningless. Instead of concentrating on the cost or the effectiveness of particular weapons (these are important issues, but secondary in nature), the strategic debate should concentrate on their capabilities and missions—

and on the strategic concepts that propel them into existence and help legitimize their approval.

FOOTNOTES

Chapter I

1. For histories of the period, see Alain Enthoven & K. Wayne Smith, *How Much Is Enough?* (NY: Harper & Row, 1971); Jerome H. Kahan, *Security in the Nuclear Age* (Washington, D.C.: Brookings Institution, 1974); William W. Kaufmann, *The McNamara Strategy* (NY: Harper & Row, 1964).

2. Enthoven & Smith, pp. 183, 210.

3. *The Military Balance 1974-1975* (London: International Institute for Strategic Studies-IISS, 1974), p. 75; Harold Brown, Department of Defense (DoD), *Annual Report FY 1980,* p. 71.

4. Enthoven & Smith, p. 207.

5. Kevin N. Lewis, *U.S. Strategic Force Structure and Employment Planning, 1959-1979* (Master's thesis, Political Science, M.I.T., 1979), p. 19.

6. Lewis is particularly persuasive on this point. See also Desmond Ball, *Deja Vu: The Return to Counterforce in the Nixon Administration* (Santa Monica, CA: California Seminar on Arms Control and Foreign Policy, 1974), p. 16.

7. See Ball, pp. 12-16.

8. *Ibid.,* p. 16.

9. Lewis and Ball are the two best; while their works are hard to find, they are very much worth tracking down.

10. Harold Brown, testimony, House Armed Services Committee, Authorization Hearings, FY 1980, Pt. 1, p. 548; and Harold Brown, testimony, Hearings, Senate Foreign Relations Committee, *The SALT II Treaty, Pt. 1,* (July 1979), p. 113. (Emphasis added.)

11. General David Jones, Hearings, Senate Armed Services Committee, Authorization Hearings, FY 1980, Pt. 1, p. 74.

12. The most eloquent defense of limited options remains one of the first: William W. Kaufmann, "The Requirements of Deterrence" and "Limited War," in Kaufmann, ed., *Military Policy and National Security* (Princeton: Princeton University Press, 1956).

13. See annual issues of *The Military Balance.*

14. A Minuteman II, of 1.2 megatons per warhead, with accuracy of about 2000 feet, has about a 70 percent chance of destroying an older Soviet silo equipped to resist blasts of up to 300 pounds per square inch (psi) overpressure. A Minuteman III, with a 335-kiloton Mk-12A warhead and accuracy of about 600 feet, has about a 70 percent chance of destroying a modern Soviet silo of 2500 psi. (Calculated on D.C. Kephart, *Damage Probability Computer for Point Targets with P and Q Vulnerability Numbers* (Santa Monica, CA: RAND Corp., 1974).

15. See James Schlesinger, DoD, *Annual Report, FY 1975* and *FY 1976* and *FY 197T;* see also his testimony in Hearings, Senate Foreign Relations Committee, *U.S. and Soviet Strategic Doctrine and Military Policies* (March 1974); and Hearings, Senate Foreign Relations Committee, *Briefing on Counterforce Attacks* (September 1974).

16. For an elaboration of Brown's "countervailing strategy," see his *Annual Report, FY 1980,* pp. 74-81; *FY 1981,* pp. 65-68. (The quote is from *FY 81,* p. 66.)

Chapter II

1. One notable exception was Murray Marder, "Carter to Inherit Intense Dispute on Soviet Intentions," *Washington Post,* January 2, 1977. For a critical analysis of Team B, see Senate Select Intelligence Committee, *The National Intelligence Estimates A-B Team Episodes Concerning Soviet Strategic Capability and Objectives* (February 1978).

2. Nitze directed or helped compose NSC-68 (the first study, written in April 1950, urging post-war American rearmament), the bomber-gap study, the Gaither Commission report (sounding the alarms for a missile gap), and others.

3. See especially Keegan's speech reprinted in *Aviation Week & Space Technology (AWST),* March 28, 1977.

4. V.D. Sokolovskiy, *Soviet Military Strategy,* 3rd ed., 1968, tr. by Harriet Fast Scott (NY: Crane Russak, 3rd ed., 1972), p. 15.

5. Richard Pipes, "Why the Soviet Union Thinks It Could Fight and Win a Nuclear War," *Commentary,* July 1977, p. 34.

6. Karl von Clausewitz, *On War,* ed. and trans. by Michael Howard & Peter Paret (Princeton: Princeton University Press, 1976), p. 95.

7. *Ibid.,* p. 92.

8. Col. B. Byely, et al., *Marxism-Leninism on War and Army* (Moscow: Progress Publishers, 1972), p. 44.

9. *Ibid.*, pp. 44, 19.

10. *Ibid.,* pp. 15, 43.

11. Editor's note in Sokolovskiy, p. 167.

12. See John Erickson, "Soviet Military Power," *Strategic Review,* Spring 1973, pp. 2-7.

13. Harold Brown, DoD, *Annual Report, FY 1981,* pp. 67, 83.

14. Lengthy excerpts from this article are reprinted and analyzed in Raymond L. Garthoff, "Mutual Deterrence and Strategic Arms Limitation in Soviet Policy," *International Security,* Summer 1978. Garthoff's article is a superb analysis of Soviet military doctrine.

15. *Ibid.*

16. See Garthoff for more examples.

17. William Colby, Hearings, Senate Foreign Relations Committee, *United States/Soviet Strategic Options* (January, March, 1977), p. 142.

18. Col. Ye. Rybkin, "The Leninist Concept of War and the Present," *Communist of the Armed Forces,* October 1973.

19. *Ibid.*

20. T.K. Jones, Hearings, Joint Committee on Defense Production, *Defense Industrial Base: Industrial Preparedness and War Survival,* (November 17, 1976), p. 185.

21. Pipes, p. 34.

22. See T.K. Jones, Hearings, House Armed Services Committee, *Civil Defense Review* (February, March, 1976); P.M.S. Blackett, *Fear, War and the Bomb* (NY: McGraw-Hill, 1949).

23. See Samuel Glasstone & Philip J. Dolan, eds., *The Effects of Nuclear Weapons* (Washington, D.C.: Departments of Defense & Energy, 3rd ed., 1977); U.S. Office of Technology Assessment, *The Effects of Nuclear War* (1979); *DCPA Attack Environmental Manual* (U.S. Defense Civil Preparedness Agency, 1973).

24. A 40-kiloton warhead has a "lethal area" of roughly 8 square miles. It would take 1,010 of these warheads to produce, on average, 5 pounds per square inch (psi) blast overpressure—enough to collapse most buildings—over the area encompassed by every Soviet city with populations greater than 100,000. There are 160 MIRV warheads in a Poseidon submarine. Assuming 90 percent reliability, seven subs could do the job; eight would be needed assuming 80 percent reliability. The U.S. has 31 Poseidon subs. [Calculated on basis of Glasstone & Dolan; and Geoffrey Kemp, "Nuclear Forces for Medium Powers," *Adelphi Papers #105, 106* (London: IISS, 1974).]

25. *Pravda,* May 9, 1975.

26. Cited in Garthoff, p. 126.

27. Harold Brown, DoD, *op. cit.,* p. 3.

28. CIA, *A Dollar Cost Comparison of Soviet and U.S. Defense,* January 1979, p. 2.

29. See Les Aspin, "How to Look at the Soviet-American Balance," *Foreign Policy,* Spring 1976.

30. CIA, *op. cit.,* p. 5. For the ruble estimate, see CIA, *Estimated Soviet Defense Spending: Trends and Prospects,* June 1978.

31. Arthur J. Alexander, Abraham S. Becker, William E. Hoehn, Jr., *The Significance of Divergent U.S.-USSR Military Expenditure* (Santa Monica, CA: RAND Corp., February 1979), p. 9.

32. See Les Aspin, "The 3 Percent Solution: NATO and the U.S. Defense Budget," *Challenge,* May-June 1979, p. 24.

33. CIA, *A Dollar Cost Comparison of Soviet and U.S. Defense Activities,* p. 5.

34. *Ibid.*

35. *Ibid.*

36. *Ibid.* The same conclusion is reached in Harold Brown, DoD, *op. cit.,* p. 73.

37. See Les Aspin, "Are We Standing Still?," *Congressional Record,* July 9, 1979.

38. *Ibid.*

39. By Aspin's calculation, the Soviet arsenal of today can destroy 4,211 hardened missile silos more than it could destroy a decade ago, while the U.S. arsenal has picked up 958 additional hard targets. This effort has cost the Soviets $24,870 million, or $5.9 million per target, while it has cost the U.S. $1,150 million, or $1.2 million per target. Thus, U.S. force improvements have been 4.9 times as cost-effective. (See *Ibid.*)

40. Derived from *The Military Balance 1978-1979,* p. 82; and *SALT II Treaty,* Memorandum on Agreed Data Base, June 1979, p. 29-30. (Does not include mothballed B-52s that U.S. will dismantle.)

41. *Ibid;* plus additional information from Dept. of Defense.

42. Senate Armed Services Committee, Authorization Hearings, FY 1979, Pt. 2, p. 1032; General George S. Brown, Joint Chiefs of Staff, *United States Military Posture for FY 1979,* p. 28.

43. Throw-weight has been pushed as an important index by Paul Nitze, esp. in "Assuring Stategic Stability in an Era of Detente," *Foreign Affairs,* January 1976.

44. Senate Armed Services Committee, Authorization Hearings, FY 1979, Pt. 9, p. 6541.

45. The SS-18, with 10 warheads of 600-kilotons each and accuracy of about 600 feet by the mid-1980s, could destroy a Minuteman silo with 81 percent probability in a single shot. The MX, with 10 warheads of 335-kilotons each and accuracy of 300 feet, could destroy a harder Soviet silo

with 97 percent probability in a single shot. (For data on weapons, see Appendix.)

46. Senate Armed Services Committee, Authorization Hearings, FY 1980, Pt. 6, p. 2826.

47. See, especially, Donald Rumsfeld, DoD, *Annual Report, FY 1977*, p. 57; *FY 1978*, p. 107; T.K. Jones, *Industrial Survival and Recovery After Attack*, commissioned by Boeing, submitted to Joint Committee on Defense Production, November 1976; Evans and Novak, "Soviet Civil Defense," *Washington Post*, June 1, 1977. In the winter of 1978-79, the scare was raised again, as the Defense Civil Preparedness Agency tried to get a substantially higher budget and as a Presidential Review Commission, which led to Presidential Decision (PD) #41, decided that civil defense is an element of the strategic balance and that budget increases ought to be made accordingly.

48. See Jones, *op. cit.*; Leon Goure, *War Survival in Soviet Strategy: USSR Civil Defense* (University of Miami, 1976); General George Keegan, interview by David Binder, *New York Times,* January 3, 1977.

49. General Daniel O. Graham, cited in Hearings, *United States/Soviet Strategic Options,* p. 163.

50. Goure, pp. 114, 118; CIA, *Soviet Civil Defense,* July 1978.

51. Stansfield Turner, Hearings, Joint Economic Committee, *Allocation of Resources in the Soviet Union and China, 1977, Pt. 3,* (June 1977), p. 26.

52. Goure, pp. 114, 118, 125.

53. "Russia's Bomb Shelters," *Newsweek,* May 23, 1977; "U.S. Estimate of Soviet Defenses Questioned in Moscow," *New York Times,* January 17, 1977.

54. A. Altunin, "The Main Direction," *Voyennye Znaniia (Military Knowledge),* October 1976.

55. See Goure's last chapter, entitled "Problems and Shortcomings."

56. Goure, p. 103.

57. *Ibid.,* p. 125.

58. T.K. Jones, Hearings, House Armed Services Committees, *Civil Defense Review,* p. 248.

59. See U.S. Arms Control and Disarmament Agency, *An Analysis of Civil Defense in Nuclear War,* December 1978.

60. T.K. Jones, *Industrial Survival and Recovery After Nuclear Attack,* pp. 17, 20.

61. CIA, *Soviet Civil Defense,* p. 10.

62. U.S. Joint Committee on Defense Production, *Civil Preparedness Review, Part II: Industrial Defense and Nuclear Attack,* April 1977, pp. 20, 68.

63. See CIA, *Soviet Economic Problems and Prospects,* July 1977, p. 8.

64. *Ibid.,* p. 9; Stansfield Turner, Hearings, Joint Economic Committee, *op. cit.,* p. 27; Harold Brown, *Annual Report, FY 1979,* p. 48.

65. John Hardt, "Summary," *Soviet Economy in a New Perspective: A Compendium of Papers Submitted to the Joint Economic Committee,* October 14, 1976, p. xvii; R.S. Mathieson, *The Soviet Union: An Economic Geography* (London: Heinemann Educ. Books, 1975), pp. 47, 63-64.

66. Cf. Les Aspin, "Soviet Civil Defense: Myth & Reality," *Arms Control Today,* September 1976; J.P. Cole & F.C. German, *A Geography of the USSR: The Background to a Planned Economy* (London: Butterworths, 2nd ed., 1970), pp. 128, 179, 187-89; Emily Jack, *et al.,* "Outlook for Soviet Energy," and Alan E. Smith, "Soviet Dependence on Siberian Resource Development," in *Soviet Economy in a New Perspective,* pp. 467, 485; Joint Committee on Defense Production, *op. cit.,* p. 67; Geoffrey Kemp, *Nuclear Forces for Medium Powers, Part I: Targets and Weapons Systems,* p. 6; Mathieson, pp. 115, 117, 128, 134, 141, 146-49, 154-56, 160-61, 167, 230, 603.

67. U.S. Office of Technology Assessment, *op. cit.,* p. 76.

68. U.S. Arms Control and Disarmament Agency, briefing on civil defense received by author.

69. Jones, *op. cit.,* p. 7.

70. Cited in Clarence Robinson, Jr., "Soviets Push for Beam Weapon," *AWST,* May 2, 1977.

71. Richard Garwin, "Charged Particle Beam Weapons?" report for Council for a Livable World, May 31, 1977; see also "Charged Particle Beams," U.S. Defense Department presentation, May 1977.

72. John Parmentola & Kosta Tsipis, "Particle-Beam Weapons," *Scientific American,* April 1979, p. 57.

73. See Garwin; and Parmentola & Tsipis, p. 63.

74. Quoted in "Soviet Energy Ray a Hoax?" UPI, *Boston Globe,* June 2, 1977; see also "Carter Sees No Evidence of Soviet Laser Beams," *New York Times,* May 4, 1977.

75. The best-known version of this scenario is laid out by Paul Nitze, "Deterring Our Deterrent," *Foreign Policy,* Winter 1976-77.

76. Quoted in James Fallows, "The Muscle-Bound Superpower," *The Atlantic,* October 1979, p. 67.

77. My favorite bomb-damage calculator is D.C. Kephart, *Damage Probability Computer for Point Targets with P and Q Vulnerability Numbers* (Santa Monica, CA: RAND Corp., 1974). You can do your own rough kill-probability calculations by pen and pocket-calculator with the aid of Lynn Etheridge Davis & Warner R. Schilling, "All You Ever Wanted to Know About MIRV and ICBM Calculations But Were Not Cleared to Ask," *Journal of Conflict Resolution,* June 1973.

78. U.S. Office of Technology Assessment, *op. cit.,* p. 3.

79. General Alton B. Slay, Hearings, House Armed Services Committee, \uthorization Hearings, FY 1979, Pt. 3, Bk. 1, p. 849.

80. For an elaboration on this point, see James L. Foster, "Essential Equivalence: What Is It and How Should It Be Measured?," *Equivalence, Sufficiency and the International Balance: 5th National Security Affairs Conference* (Ft. McNair, Washington, D.C.: National Defense University, 1978), esp. pp. 33-43.

81. Hearings, House Armed Services Committee, *op. cit.,* p. 335; see also John D. Steinbruner & Thomas M. Garwin, "Strategic Vulnerability: The Balance Between Prudence and Paranoia," *International Security,* Summer 1976, p. 163; Lt. Col. Joseph J. McGlinchey & Dr. Jakob W. Seelig, "Why ICBMs Can Survive," *Air Force,* September 1974.

82. See Foster, *op. cit.,* p. 34; Steinbruner & Garwin, *op. cit.,* pp. 154-56; Senate Armed Services Committee, Authorization Hearings, FY 1979, Pt. 9, p. 6481; Kosta Tsipis, *Nuclear Explosion Effects on Missile Silos* (Cambridge, MA: M.I.T. Center for International Studies, February 1978).

83. For evidence suggesting that the U.S. may be leaning toward a launch-on-warning/launch-under-attack posture, see House Armed Services Committee, Authorization Hearings, FY 1979, Pt. 1, p. 960; Senate Armed Services Committee, Authorization Hearings, FY 1979, Pt. 2, p. 1123.

84. Harold Brown, Hearings, House Armed Services Committee, *op. cit.,* p. 64.

85. The U.S. has about 9,486 total warheads, of which 2154 are on ICBMs.

86. Harold Brown, Hearings, Senate Foreign Relations Committee, *The SALT II Treaty, Pt. 1* (July 1979), p. 301 (Emphasis added).

87. Harold Brown, DoD, *Annual Report, FY 79,* p. 53; *FY 1980,* p. 76; Harold Brown, Hearings, Senate Foreign Relations, *op. cit.,* p. 113.

88. See Hearings, Senate Foreign Relations Committee, *Analyses of Effects of Limited Nuclear Warfare* (September 1975); U.S. Office of Technology Assessment, *op. cit.*

89. See Nitze, "Deterring Our Deterrent"; and much of the literature of the Committee on the Present Danger.

90. Senate Armed Services Committee, Authorization Hearings, FY 1979, Pt. 9, p. 6538.

91. Robert Soule & Richard Davison, Congressional Budget Office, *The MX Missile and Multiple Protective Structure Basing: Long-Term Budget Implications* (June 1979), p. 131; Harold Brown, speech before Council on Foreign Relations, April 5, 1979 (reprinted in *Congressional Record,* April 5, 1979, p. S4089).

92. U.S. Air Force, letter to Rep. Les Aspin, November 2, 1978.

93. *SALT II Agreement,* Art. IV, Sec. 10 (June 18, 1979).

94. Dr. William Perry, Hearings, Senate Armed Services Committee, *FY 1979 Supplemental Authorization* (Feb., March, April, 1979), pp. 101, 197.

95. CIA, *Estimated Soviet Defense Spending: Trends and Prospects,* p. 3.

96. Cited by Harold Brown, Hearings, Senate Foreign Relations Committee, *The SALT II Treaty, Pt. 1* (July 1979), p. 351.

97. Philip Klass, "Pentagon Analyzes Test of Tomahawk," *AWST,* November 20, 1978, p. 24; "Perry Confirms Soviet Look-Down Tests," *AWST,* January 1, 1979, p. 17; Coleman Rogers, "B52 Role Facing Change: Cruise Missile Test Results," *Military Electronics/Countermeasures,* February 1979, p. 107; Senate Armed Services Committee, Authorization Hearings, FY 1979, Pt. 2, pp. 1003-04.

98. The phrase is from Herbert York, *Race to Oblivion* (NY: Simon & Schuster, 1971).

99. See House Armed Services Committee, Authorization Hearings, FY 1980, Pt. I, pp. 1180-1206, 1248-55.

Chapter III

1. See Aspin, "Are We Standing Still?"

2. A.A. Tinajero, Congressional Research Service, *The MX Intercontinental Ballistic Missile Program* (Issue Brief 1B77080, July 27, 1977).

3. "New Propellant Evaluated for Trident Second Stage," *AWST,* October 13, 1975, pp. 16-17; Trident II will be a hard-target killer (See Harold Brown, DoD, *Annual Report, FY 1979,* p. 114.).

4. For great double-talk on this, see Harold Brown, DoD, *Annual Report, FY 1980,* p. 77.

5. See Appendix.

6. U.S. Defense Advanced Research Projects Agency, *FY 1978 Program for Research and Development,* February 1977, p. I3.12-14, I122.30.

7. To get out into the Atlantic Ocean, the Soviet subs must traverse a fairly narrow gap of water between Greenland and Iceland and between Iceland and the United Kingdom (called G-I-UK Gap). The U.S. has sensors and ASW equipment all along this stretch of ocean. For material on overwhelming superiority of the U.S. in the area of anti-submarine warfare (ASW), see Senate Armed Services Committee, Authorization Hearings, FY 1979, Pt. 9, pp. 6662-67; *Ibid.,* Pt. 2, pp. 1038, 1041, 1121-2; and Bruce Blair, "Arms Control Implications of Anti-submarine Warfare (ASW) Programs," in Congressional Research Service, *Evaluationon of Fiscal Year 1979 Arms Control Impact Statements,* report to House International Relations Committee (January 3, 1979) pp 103-19.

8. Senate Armed Services Committee, Authorization Hearings, FY80, Pt. 6, p. 2841.

9. See Hearings, House Armed Services Committee, *Civil Defense Review,* pp. 7-8, 60, 118, 290.

10. Byely, *et al., op. cit.,* p. 41.

11. See *The Military Balance, 1979-1980* (London: IISS, 1979), pp. 114-19.

Chapter IV

1. See Fred M. Kaplan, "SALT: The End of Arms Control," *The Progressive,* January 1978, p. 22.

2. G.W. Rathjens, Abram Chayes & J.P. Ruina, *Nuclear Arms Control Agreements: Process and Impact* (Washington, D.C.: Carnegie Endowment for International Peace, 1974), p. 21. This monograph is one of the earliest, and still the most compelling, analyses of SALT's counterproductive tendencies.

3. See particularly the statements of Sen. McGovern, Proxmire and Hatfield in *Congressional Record,* March 5, 1979, pp. S2041, 2042, 2046; Richard Egan, "3 Senators Hold Key to Arms Pact," *Detroit News,* July 5, 1979; Fred Barbash, "3 Liberals Assail Concessions to SALT Critics," *Washington Post,* March 5, 1979.

4. For an elaboration of this view, see Les Aspin, "The Third Position: SALT II and Its Liberal Critics," *Congressional Record,* July 23, 1979.

5. *Ibid.;* William Perry, Hearings, Senate Armed Services Committee, Authorization Hearings, FY 1980, Pt. 3, pp. 1411, 1431; Michael Getler and Robert Kaiser, "Intelligence Estimate Said to Show Need for SALT," *Washington Post,* January 31, 1980.

6. David G. Hoag, "Strategic Ballistic Missile Guidance—A Story of Ever Greater Accuracy." *Astronautics & Aeronautics,* May 1978, p. 38.

7. Dr. Sidney Drell, director of the Stanford Linear Accelerator Center, is reportedly the originator of this idea, and Harold Brown seemed intrigued by the notion. See Strobe Talbott, *Endgame: The Inside Story of SALT II* (NY: Harper and Row, 1979), p. 55.

8. See *Ibid.,* pp. 207-8.

9. Senate Armed Services Committee Authorization Hearings, FY 1975, Pt. 7, p. 3920.

10. "Soviets Test Killer Spacecraft," *AWST,* October 30, 1978; Walter Pincus, "U.S. Seeks One-Year Satellite-Killer Test Ban," *Washington Post,* April 11, 1979.

11. Senate Armed Services Committee, Authorization Hearings, FY 1980, Pt. VI, pp. 3016-18; "The New Military Race in Space," *Business Week,* June 4, 1979, p. 145.

12. This was devised by Jeremy J. Stone, director of the Federation of

American Scientists in Washington, DC. See his "An Arms Race in Reverse," *Washington Post,* December 31, 1978.

Chapter V

1. See Aspin, "Are We Standing Still?"

2. William T. Lee, "Soviet Military Policy: Objectives and Capabilities," *Air Force,* March 1979, p. 54.

3. For example, in the 3rd edition of *Military Strategy,* published in 1968, Marshall Sokolovskiy writes: " . . . possibilities of averting a surprise attack are constantly growing. Present means of reconnaissance, detection and surveillance can opportunely disclose a significant portion of the measures of direct preparation of a nuclear attack by the enemy and in the very first minutes locate the mass launch of missiles and the take-off of aircraft belonging to be aggressor and, at the right time, warn the political leadership of the country about the impending danger. Thus, possibilities exist not to allow a surprise attack by an aggressor, to deliver nuclear strikes on him at the right time" (p. 280). This strongly suggests the possibility of launch-on-warning.

4. On rapid retargeting, see Donald Rumsfeld, DoD, *Annual Report, FY 1978,* p. 124.

5. Harold Brown has said: " . . . whatever doubts one may have about whether a nuclear war could be kept limited—and I have serious ones—it would be the height of folly to put the United States in a position in which uncontrolled escalation would be the only course we could follow." (Hearings, Sen. Foreign Relations Committee, *The SALT II Treaty, Vol. 1,* p. 113.) There is certainly something to this point.

6. Defense Secretary James Schlesinger is chiefly responsible for linking limited options and counterforce together. For an excellent analysis that supports the former but remains skeptical of the latter, see Lynn Etheridge Davis, *Limited Nuclear Options: Deterrence and the New American Doctrine,* Adelphi Paper #121 (London: IISS, 1976).

Chapter VI

1. For detailed analysis on this point, see Aspin, "Are We Standing Still?"

2. Edward Luttwak, "Perceptions of Military Force and U.S. Defense Policy," *Survival,* January/February 1977, p. 3.

3. Admiral Stansfield Turner, "The Naval Balance: Not Just a Numbers Game," *Foreign Affairs,* January 1977, p. 346.

APPENDIX:
U.S. AND SOVIET STRATEGIC WEAPONS AND PLANS FOR THE 1980s

U.S. (as of 1/80)

System	(a) First Deployed	(b) Delivery Vehicles	(c) Weapons Load (Warheads x Yield)	(d) Total Warheads	(e) (naut. mi.) CEP	(f) Silo Kill-Probability 1-shot	2-shot
ICBM							
Titan II	1962	54	1 x 9 Mt	54	.7	.11	.21
Minuteman II	1966	450	1 x 1.2 Mt	450	.3	.27	.31
Minuteman III/Mk-12	1970	540	3 x 170 Kt (MIRV)	1,620	.1	.55	.80
Minuteman III/Mk-12A	12/79	10	3 x 335 Kt (MIRV)	30	.1	.70	.91
SLBM							
Polaris	1964	160	3 x 200 Kt (MRV)	160	.5	.08	.15
Poseidon	1970	480	9 x 40 Kt (MIRV)	4,320	.25	.05	.10
Trident I	1979	16	8 x 100 Kt (MIRV)	128	.25	.10	.19
Bombers							
B-52D	1956	79	4 x 1.2 Mt	316	.1	.94	.99
B-52G	1959	173	4 x 1.2 Mt + SRAM	692	.1	.94	.99
B-52H	1961	96	4 x 1.2 Mt + SRAM	384	.1	.94	.99
FB-111	1969	66	2 x 1.2 Mt + SRAM	132	.1	.94	.99
			+ 1200 SRAM	1,200			
TOTAL		2,124		9,486			

SOURCES:

(a) Date for Minuteman III/Mk-12A warhead from U.S. Air Force; for Trident I, from Harold Brown, DoD, *Annual Report, FY 1981,* p. 131; all others from *The Military Balance 1979-1980* (London: International Institute for Strategic Studies, 1979), pp. 86, 88.

(b) ICBM and SLBM numbers from Harold Brown, DoD, *op. cit.,* pp. 72-73. Bomber estimate is for Total Active Inventory; breakdowns are from U.S. Air Force, information provided to author.

SLBMs break down as follows: All Polaris missiles in 10 Polaris submarines; the Poseidons in 30 Poseidon submarines; the Trident I's in one Poseidon submarine.

(c) Weapon loads assume average, not maximum, loading of warheads per missile. MIRV indicates Multiple Independently target-able Re-entry Vehicles; MRV indicates Multiple Re-Entry Vehicles that are all aimed at the same area; hence, each MIRV counts as a separate warhead, the warheads on an MRV platform count only as a single warhead.

Numbers from Les Aspin, "The Mineshaft Gap Revisited," *Congressional Record,* January 15, 1979, p. E30.

(d) The product of (b) times number of warheads listed in (c). (MRVs count as one warhead, though.)

(e) Circular Error Probable, or the distance in nautical-miles within which a warhead will land from the target 50% of the time. Numbers from Aspin, *op. cit.*

(f) Assumes targets are Soviet silos of 2500 pounds-per-square-inch (psi) blast resistance. The figure does not include degradation due to less-than-100% reliability; that is, in real life, the number would be lower. One-shot calculated on D.C. Kephart, *Damage Probability Computer for Point Targets with P and Q Vulnerability Numbers* (Santa Monica, Ca: RAND Corp., 1974), and Kephart, "VNTK Adjustment Monograph for P-type Targets," supplied to author. 2-shot figure is derived by calculating $1 - (1-Pk)^2$ where Pk=single-shot kill-probability.

It must be noted that many experts believe that two-on-one firing tactics are physically impossible—or at least highly improbable to execute—because of the phenomenon known as "fratricide."

USSR (as of 1/80)

System	(a) First Deployed	(b) Delivery Vehicles	(c) Weapons Load (Warheads x Yield)	(d) Total Warheads	(e) CEP	(f) Silo Kill-Probability 1-shot	2-shot
ICBM							
SS-9	1965	61	1 x 15 Mt	61	.7	.19	.34
SS-11	1966	}639	1 x 1 Mt	}639	.7	.06	.12
Mod. 3	1973		3 x 500 Kt (MRV)		.5	.12	.23
SS-13	1968	60	1 x 1 Mt	60	.7	.06	.12
SS-17							
Mod 1	1977	130	4 x 750 Kt (MIRV)	520	.25	.34	.56
Mod 2	1977	20	1 x 3 Mt	20	.25	.57	.82
SS-18							
Mod 1 & 3	1975/76	26	1 x 20 Mt	26	.25	.97	.99
Mod 2	1976	171	8 x 750 Kt (MIRV)	1,368	.25	.34	.56
Mod 4	1979	50	10 x 600 Kt (MIRV)	500	.15	.59	.83
SS-19							
Mod 1	1976	211	6 x 550 Kt (MIRV)	1,266	.15	.58	.82
Mod 2	1976	30	1 x 3 Mt	30	.25	.61	.85
SLBM							
SS-N-5	1964	18	1 x 1 Mt	18	1.5	.01	.02
SS-N-6	1968	468	1 x 1 Mt	468	1.5	.01	.02
SS-N-8	1973	289	1 x 1 Mt	289	.8	.05	.10
SS-N-17	1979	12	1 x 750 Kt	12	.5	.10	.19
SS-N-18	1978	160	3 x 500 Kt (MIRV)	480	.5	.16	.29
Bombers							
Bear	1956	113	2 x 1-5 Mt	226	.2	.52-.83	.77-.97
Bison	1956	43	2 x 1-5 Mt	86	.2	.52-.83	.77-.97
TOTAL		2,501					

SOURCES:

(a) Date of SS-18 Mod-4 from U.S. Defense Department; all others from *The Military Balance 1979-1980* (London: International Institute for Strategic Studies, 1979), p. 87.

(b) ICBM numbers derived from Congressional Research Service, "Reducing the Number of U.S. and Soviet Strategic Offensive Weapons: An Analysis of Two SALT III Options Based on the SALT II Ceilings," *Congressional Record,* October 31, 1979, p. S15565. This source provides data as of June 1979; I've extrapolated to January 1980, using Soviet production rate of 125 MIRVed ICBMs per year (as frequently quoted by Harold Brown) and assuming that this production rate was distributed among the various individual ICBMs in the past six months as it had been in prior years. This source also divides SS-18 only into MIRVed and non-MIRVed, not making distinctions between Mod-2 and Mod-4. I estimate 50 Mod-4s on the following basis: Secretary Brown has testified that the Soviets began deploying 10-warhead versions of the SS-18 only in 1979 (testimony on SALT II, before Senate Foreign Relations Committee, September 19, 1979; reprinted in *Congressional Record,* October 4, 1979, p. S14117); the Mod-4 is the 10-warhead version; I assume that all SS-18s produced in the past year were Mod-4 versions.

SLBM numbers from Col. (ret.) John Collins, Library of Congress, generally a reliable source for such raw data. The breakdown is as follows: four SS-N-6s on Golf-IV subs and 464 on Yankee-I's; for SS-N-8, six on Golf-III, three on Hotel-III, 216 on Delta-I, 64 on Delta-II subs; SS-N-17s on Yankee-II subs; SS-N-18s on Delta-IIIs.

Bomber numbers from *The Military Balance 1979-1980,* p. 89.

(c) Weapon Load from Paul Nitze, testimony, Senate Foreign Relations Committee, *The SALT II Treaty, Pt. 1,* p. 458; Walter Pincus, "U.S. Downgrades Soviet ICBM Yield," *Washington Post,* May 31, 1979; *Aviation Week & Space Technology,* October 17, 1977, p. 15.

(d) CEP from Nitze, *op. cit.; Aviation Week & Space Technology,* April 18, 1977, p. 18.

(f) Assumes targets are U.S. silos of 2000 pounds-per-square-inch (psi) blast resistance. For further details and assumptions, see note (f) of table on U.S. strategic forces.

The 1980s

The United States

ICBMs—By 1982, the United States will have placed Mk-12A warheads on 300 of its 550 Minuteman III ICBMs. In 1986, the M-X is scheduled to go into initial deployment, with all 200 fielded by the end of the decade. Each missile will have up to 14 warheads, each with 335 to 500 kilotons, depending on whether the Mk-12A or Advanced Ballistic Re-Entry Vehicle (ABRV) is used as a warhead. (If just ABRV is used, M-X could hold at most ten.) M-X will also have an Advanced Inertial Reference Sphere (AIRS) guidance system, giving it accuracy of roughly 300 feet CEP. With a Mk-12A, each M-X warhead would have theoretically 97 percent single-shot kill-probability against a hardened Soviet missile silo; with ABRV, about a 99 percent probability.

SLBMs—By 1982, all ten Polaris subs will have been phased out (half will be converted to attack submarines). At the same time, Trident I's will have been backfitted into 12 of our 31 Poseidon submarines. In 1981, the first Trident sub will enter the sea; one a year will be produced through 1985 and, after that point, three every two years. One Trident sub will hold 192 warheads—more than in all the Polaris subs combined. By the late 1980s, the United States might field Trident II missiles for the Trident subs, each holding up to 14 warheads of 150 kilotons each, with accuracy of about 300 feet, giving it very high hard-target kill-capability.

Bombers—Beginning in 1983, the Air-Launched Cruise Missile (ALCM) wil be placed onto B-52G bombers, with 120 of these planes equipped by 1982 and 152 of them loaded with 3,040 ALCMs by the end of the decade. Each ALCM explodes with 150 kilotons of power, and can land within 100 to 300 feet of its target, due to a Terrain-contour Matching computer guidance system (TERCOM). With such accuracy, it should be able to destroy virtually anything aimed at. Meanwhile, a Cruise Missile Carrier Aircraft of some type will be entering the arsenal by the end of the decade—holding between 20 and 60 ALCMs each, depending on which type of plane the Air Force chooses. At this writing, the Air Force and much of Congress wants the Strategic Weapons Launcher to serve as the ALCM-carrier; this plane is a fixed-wing version of the B-1 bomber.

The Soviet Union

ICBMs—Over the next few years, SS-18s will continue to replace SS-9s, and SS-17s and SS-19s will continue to be fitted into SS-11 silos as the older missiles are discarded. About 125 of these newer missiles will probably be deployed each year through 1985. If SALT II is enacted, the Soviets will probably have, by 1985, 200 Ss-17s, 308 SS-18s, and 312 SS-19s. If there is no SALT II, they will probably still have 308 SS-18s, but potentially many more SS-17s and SS-19s. Accuracy on the SS-18 and SS-19 will probably be 600 feet by 1985, giving them kill-probabilities of 85 and 84 percent, respectively, in one shot (not including reliability flaws). A new generation of ICBMs currently is in early R&D; they are probably replacements for all the MIRV missiles and a new light single-warhead replacement for the SS-11. Their characteristics are as yet unknown.

SLBMs—Much depends on whether SALT II is ever ratified by the U.S. Senate. Even now, the Soviets could be producing and deploying more submarines, but the SALT II ceilings, which they have already reached, constrict them. Assuming SALT II, the Soviets could have about 380 SS-N-18-type SLBMs (then with seven, not three, MIRV warheads) and about 470 single-warhead SLBMs; without SALT II, they could have several more. Soon, the Soviets will put to sea their newest submarine, the Typhoon, which, like the U.S. Trident, holds 24 missiles.

Bombers—The Soviets are doing less here. The controversial Backfire bomber continues to be produced at a rate of about 30 per year; it has limited intercontinental capability, but is almost universally believed to be intended for anti-ship and "theater" missions (e.g., against Europe or Asia, not the United States). Some reports allege that the Soviets are building a new heavy bomber, similar to the B-1; but no hard evidence indicates this as yet.

IPS PUBLICATIONS

Research Guide to Current Military and Strategic Affairs
William M. Arkin

The first comprehensive and authoritative reference to national security issues. Cites and evaluates all basic research tools. Indispensable for information on the U.S. military establishment, the defense budget, arms sales and military aid, weapons systems, NATO, arms control and disarmament, Soviet military affairs, global strategic issues, and intelligence operations.

"This is more than a bibliography—the author has used his background in defense analysis to produce a guide to worldwide information sources ... The book has a feature not often included in such guides, names and addresses of sources for specific kinds of information ... The choice of sources is more than adequate, and the writing and arrangement are both excellent ... No single volume takes its place."

Library Journal

"Arkin's work is a veritable mine of information on military organization, infrastructure, and operations ... Rarely is a research tool so complete and useful."

Le Monde Diplomatique

"This excellent guide will be helpful to the advanced student/researcher wishing information not limited to the available published literature ... Arkin describes the organizations generating the information in this field and informs the researcher of offices to consult and legal devices available to gain information."

Choice

"In short, Arkin has done us all a service."

Arms Control Today

$15.95 ($7.95 paper)

Beyond the "Vietnam Syndrome"
U.S. Interventionism in the 1980s
Michael T. Klare
Foreword by Richard J. Barnet

"Is America heading toward new foreign military adventures? Klare answers, "Yes, " in this important study of U.S. military policy in the 1980s. The country is recovering from the isolationist syndrome caused by the Vietnam experience, especially in the higher levels of defense planning ... This collection of articles reviews the growth of the Rapid Deployment Force, examines plans made to insure that we continue to receive Middle Eastern oil, and studies the rebirth of counterinsurgency doctrine. The book demonstrates Klare's expertise in defense studies and is clearly written and documented. This important book should be in most libraries."

Library Journal

"Michael Klare's essays make important reading in the Reagan years. He traces the evolution of the so-called Vietnam Syndrome and shows how the offficial attitudes in Washington have veered once more in the direction of armed intervention."

Richard J. Barnet
Author, *Real Security*

$4.95

Soviet Policy in the Arc of Crisis
Fred Halliday

The crescent of nations extending from Ethiopia through the Arab world to Iran and Afghanistan has become the setting of an intense new geopolitical drama.

"Halliday's newest book expertly deflates all the new Cold War myths surrounding Soviet intentions and capabilities in "Arc of Crisis," whether it be Afghanistan, Iran, or the Horn of Africa. It is essential reading in the Reagan era."

Kai Bird
The Nation

"Finally there is a book available that measures the allegations of Soviet intervention in the Middle East against the facts. I doubt if any publication could be more timely than Fred Halliday's lucid exposition of the realities of Soviet involvement in the region. Halliday's work is an implicit indictment of the U.S. media's failure to scrutinize the distortions orchestrated from Washington and deserves the widest possible circulation in any effort to head off further U.S. military escalation in the Middle East."

Joe Stork
MERIP Reports

$4.95

Supplying Repression
U.S. Support for Authoritarian Regimes Abroad
Michael T. Klare and Cynthia Arnson with Delia Miller and Daniel Volman
Introduction by Richard Falk

A detailed analysis of the programs—police, military, and commercial—through which the U.S. delivers repressive arms, technology, and expertise to Third World regimes directly engaged in political terrorism and the suppression of dissent. Klare and Arnson argue that supplying repression has been a consistent characteristic of U.S. foreign policy since the origins of the Cold War, with the "national security syndrome" serving as the rationale for bolstering dictatorships around the globe.

"More fully and convincingly than anywhere else, Klare and Arnson, with dispassionate precision and attention to detail, depict the profiles of this distinctively American Gulag."

Richard Falk
Princeton University

"Very important, fully documented indictment of U.S. role in supplying rightist Third World governments with the weaponry and know-how of repression."

The Nation

$9.95 ($4.95 paper)

Real Security: Restoring American Power in a Dangerous Decade
Richard J. Barnet

"*Real Security* is a *tour de force,* a gift to the country. One of the most impassioned and effective arguments for sanity and survival that I have ever read."

Dr. Robert L. Heilbroner

"An inspired and inspiring achievement ... a first salvo in the campaign to turn our current security policies—diplomatic, military, and economic—in the direction of rationality. It may well be the basic statement around which opponents of unalloyed confrontation can gather. It will have great impact."

John Marshall Lee
Vice Admiral, USN (Ret.)

"As a summary of the critical literature on the arms race, Barnet's brief essay is an important antidote to hawkish despair."

Kirkus Reviews

$10.95 ($4.95 paper)

Dubious Specter
A Skeptical Look at the Soviet Nuclear Threat
Fred M. Kaplan

Do the Soviets really threaten American ICBMs with a devastating surprise attack? Will Soviet military doctrine lead the Russians to threaten nuclear war in order to wring concessions from the West? Do Soviet leaders think they can fight and win a nuclear war?

"In this concise, well-balanced fact-packed volume, Fred Kaplan has laid out the issues and the realities of the current Soviet-American nuclear confrontation ... and outlines a prudent and sensible policy of reasonable strength, unilateral U.S. actions and prudent arms control aspirations ..."

Bernard T. Feld, Editor-in-Chief
The Bulletin of the Atomic Scientists

"Fred Kaplan's precise, detailed analysis is a valuable tool for the main task in national defense policy—distinguishing between the weapons that are crucial to our security and those that, like the Maginot Line, consume our resources and weaken real defense."

James Fallows
The Atlantic Monthly

"An important addition to the literature on the U.S./U.S.S.R. strategic balance."

Herbert Scoville
The Arms Control Association

$4.95

Resurgent Militarism
Michael T. Klare and the Bay Area Chapter
of the Inter-University Committee

An analysis of the origins and consequences of the growing militaristic fervor which is spreading from Washington across the nation. The study examines America's changing strategic position since Vietnam and the political and economic forces which underlie the new upsurge in militarism.
$2.00

The Counterforce Syndrome
A Guide to U.S. Nuclear Weapons and Strategic Doctrine
Robert C. Aldridge

This study discloses the shift from "deterrence" to "counter-force" in U.S. strategic doctrine. Former Trident engineer Robert Aldridge presents a thorough summary and analysis of U.S. strategic nuclear weapons and military policy including descriptions of MIRVs, MARVs, Trident systems, cruise missiles, and MX missiles in relation to the aims of a U.S. first strike attack.

"The superpowers are putting a hair trigger on their nuclear missiles. *The Counterforce Syndrome* explains why this new nuclear policy undermines American security and threatens human survival in the 1980s."

George McGovern

"Essential reading for those who want to stop this dangerously irrational policy."

Arthur Macy Cox

$4.95

The Rise and Fall of the "Soviet Threat"
Domestic Sources of the Cold War Consensus
Alan Wolfe

Summarizing the history of the Cold War from 1948 to the present, Wolfe suggests that American fear of the Soviet Union tends to fluctuate according to domestic factors as well as in relation to the military and foreign policies of the USSR. Wolfe contends that recurring features of American domestic politics periodically coalesce to spur anti-Soviet sentiment, contributing to increased tensions and dangerous confrontations.

"At this moment, one could hardly want a more relevant book."
Kirkus Reviews

$4.95

A Continent Besieged
Foreign Military Activities in Africa Since 1975
Daniel Volman

A study of the growing military involvement of the two superpowers and their allies in Africa.
$2.00

Assassination on Embassy Row
John Dinges and Saul Landau

A devastating political document that probes all aspects of the Letelier-Moffitt assassinations, interweaving the investigations of the murder by the FBI and the Institute. The story surpasses the most sophisticated fiction in depth of characterization at the same time that it raises serious and tantalizing questions about the response of American intelligence and foreign policy to international terrorism.

" ... An engrossing study of international politics and subversion ... "

Kirkus Reviews

" ... A superb spy thriller ... "

Newsweek

~~$14.95~~ SPECIAL OFFER $5.95

The Nicaraguan Revolution
A Personal Report
Richard R. Fagan

Tracing the history of the Nicaraguan Revolution, Fagen focuses on six legacies that define current Nicaraguan reality: armed struggle; internationalization of the conflict; national unity; democratic visions; death, destruction and debts; and political bankruptcy. This primer on the state of Nicaraguan politics and economics provides an insightful view of the Sandinist quest for power and hegemony. The report contains twenty photographs by Marcelo Montecino and appendices with the basic documents necessary for understanding contemporary Nicaraguan affairs.
$4.00

Chile: Economic 'Freedom'
and Political Repression
Orlando Letelier

A trenchant analysis by the former leading official of the Allende government who was assassinated by the Pinochet junta. This essay demonstrates the necessary relationship between an economic development model which benefits only the wealthy few and the political terror which has reigned in Chile since the overthrow of the Allende regime. Appendix with 1980 socioeconomic indicators.
$1.00

Decoding Corporate Camouflage
U.S. Business Support for Apartheid
Elizabeth Schmidt
Foreword by Congressman Ronald Dellums

By exposing the decisive role of U.S. corporations in sustaining apartheid, this study places highly-touted employment "reforms" in the context of the systematic economic exploitation and political repression of the black South African majority.

" ... forcefully presented."

Kirkus Reviews

$4.95

South Africa
Foreign Investment and Apartheid
Lawrence Litvak, Robert DeGrasse,
and Kathleen McTigue

A critical examination of the argument that multinationals and foreign investment operate as a force for progressive change in South Africa.

"Its concise and well-documented debunking of the myth that foreign investment will eventually change the system of exploitation and repression in South Africa deserves wide readership ... Highly recommended."

Library Journal

$4.95

Feeding the Few
Corporate Control of Food
Susan George

The author of *How the Other Half Dies* has extended her critique of the world food system which is geared towards profit not people. This study draws the links between the hungry at home and those abroad exposing the economic and political forces pushing us towards a unified global food system.
$4.95

Postage and Package:
All orders must be prepaid. For delivery within the USA, please add 15% of order total. For delivery outside the USA, add 20%. Standard discounts available upon request.

Please write the Institute for Policy Studies, 1901 Q Street, N.W., Washington, D.C. 20009 for our complete catalog of publications and films.